livelifeonpurpose

God's Purpose.   Your Life.   One Journey.

livelifeonpurpose

God's Purpose.   Your Life.   One Journey.

claude hickman
foreword by todd ahrend

WINEPRESS WP PUBLISHING

Packaged by WinePress Publishing, PO Box 428, Enumclaw, WA 98022. The views expressed or implied in this work do not necessarily reflect those of WinePress Publishing. The author(s) is ultimately responsible for the design, content and editorial accuracy of this work.

10/40 Window map provided by GMI. Italics, bold, or underlined in the Biblical text is added by the author for emphasis.

All scriptures are taken from the New American Standard Bible, © 1960, 1963, 1968, 1971, 1972, 1973, 1975, 1977 by The Lockman Foundation. Used by permission.

ISBN 1-57921-826-1
Library of Congress Catalog Card Number: 2003112031

contents

Thank You

To my wife Rebecca, who has chosen to live her life on purpose and walk the journey with me as a faithful, honest, and loving friend. God has blessed me with a companion to travel the journey with like Jonathan's armor–bearer who said, *"Do all that is in your heart; turn yourself, and here I am with you according to your desire."*

To my parents who have been steadfast support in all I do. And to John, Todd, Sean, Ted, Steve, and Neil; the men that God has used to direct my life toward the true treasure.

To Grace Baptist Church, where we have learned the meaning of true worship, fellowship, and community—especially to Jim and Jason for leading us in truth and authenticity.

To all our supporters, who live their lives on purpose, faithfully investing in the work of the Lord through us and our ministry year after year. Each of them are directly responsible for this book and any fruit that comes from it.

"A prophet to his own generation, Claude points his readers to the true North Star and challenges them to a journey that will make a world of difference."

– Bill Jones , Columbia International University professor, writer, speaker, and president of Crossover Communications mission agency.

foreword
By Todd Ahrend

Most people want to live for something. It is rare to meet a person who doesn't want to live for anything; someone with no ambitions, drive, goals, or intentions. People crave purpose. We want to be a part of something that will outlast us. We all want, at the end of the day—and more importantly at the end of our lives, to be able to say, "I contributed to something ... I made an impact on those lives... I spent my time in significance." As believers, God has invited us into His purpose. We actually have the ability to live for something beyond ourselves; something global! Many times though, this potential is not realized in believers' lives. Whatever the reason, be it lack of information, unwillingness to seek Him, or fear of what we must do when He reveals Himself, we seek instant gratification for our purpose craving, so we jump on the first opportunity that comes along. I know in my own life this is true. When I first became a believer, I sought zealously all that I perceived to be the Christian life. I tossed all my secular music, put motivating stickers on my car, and even tried to evangelize by wearing the most Christian t-shirts I could find. I thought all this was what it meant to be a good Christian. But the more I grew spiritually the more I realized that God was not really interested in me Christianizing my life as much as He was interested in me crucifying my life. The problem that many of us face is that when we become Christians we simply adjust all of our natural ambition toward Christian things. Whatever effort we put toward the pursuit of carnal goals before Christ is now spent in pursuit of Christianized goals. Not much changes. It seems from scripture, however, that God is challenging us to lay down our ambitions. Not simply to adjust them but to abandon our ambitions in exchange for His. In order for this great exchange to take place a few things have to happen. First, you must crucify your life to Him. Second, you have to know what His ambitions are. And third, you have to know practically how you are going to live out His goals. These steps are the reasons Claude Hickman wrote this book.

The heartbeat of the book *Live Life on Purpose* is to give a challenging call to all who seek to crucify their lives to the Lord, and to offer a blueprint of what a life full of purpose could look like. Not only does Claude walk you through scripture and give a thorough explanation of the global purpose of God, but he also goes step by step through some practical applications of what the life lived on purpose will cost you. You will be convinced and stirred for God's desire and plan to use you in His grandest endeavor—an endeavor that He promises will touch all nations.

Claude Hickman serves as a genuine example of a life lived on purpose. Over the years, I have watched him say no to some very good, very safe, even appealing opportunities, and I've seen him throw off everything that hinders and the sin that so easily entangles and run with perseverance the race marked out before him. The book you are holding is not just empty facts or good ideas that you might want to consider. This is a passionate cry from the author not to settle for the status quo any longer. He is not asking you to do something he himself has not yet done. As you read this book, let the Lord challenge and convict you to surrender at His feet all that you are, all that you desire, and the life you could potentially live in exchange for all that He is, all that He desires, and a life lived on purpose.

"I have been crucified with Christ and I no longer live, but Christ lives in me ..." (Gal 2:20).

Our Journey

"I will not follow where the path may lead; but I will go where there is no path; and I will leave a trail..."

– Muriel Strode

CHAPTER ONE

The Journey

the outer court

In August 2002 my wife, Rebecca, and I took a short trip to China. We were in Beijing, where all the world famous attractions are. We visited all the legendary sites and plenty of markets all in about a day. It was like the Griswald's Chinese vacation on steroids. Seriously, we stayed at the Great Wall for 45 minutes, Tiananmen Square for 30 minutes, and the Emperor's Palace for about 20 minutes. We were really flying, but we had this great taxi guy who got us around and told us how to get the most out of each sight. Our last visit was the Forbidden City. It was huge. He dropped us off on one side of this palace type structure with massive walls that surrounded it and told us he would be waiting for us on the other side (about a mile away). It is the center of Beijing and the highlight of our trip. I remember him saying, "Be sure to get in before 4 o'clock or it will close." It was 3:30—no problem. He took off; so we bought a new roll of film, took some pictures out front, and then entered through the massive arching doorway.

The Forbidden City is a series of brick courtyards, and if you keep walking straight you will keep passing through these huge doorways into another and another massive courtyard. By the time we got to the third courtyard, which was the biggest we had seen, we decided to stop and check out some souvenir carts. After a few minutes we moved on and some friendly college girls stopped my wife and practiced their English on us. Then they wanted a picture with us. We chatted a little, then left. We took some more pictures. "This is awesome," I said, "It doesn't get any better than this!" We strolled on at a swift pace through the rest of this courtyard, because we would have to make good time to meet our taxi guy on the other side at 5 p.m. and it was already 4:15. I noticed that there were doorways on the sides of the courtyard and cars driving through and I thought to myself—that's odd. What's so forbidden about this city? When we got to the next huge wall I noticed that there was no huge doorway, only a small, as in people–can–only–walk–one–way–type tunnel. "That must be the 'out' tunnel," I thought, because there were only people exiting from the other side. "Let's go," I said to Rebecca, thinking I could slip us in if we walked confidently. (After all, we are Americans!) Well, it didn't work that day. There seem to be a lot of people in China that know the word "closed." Then I remembered the words of our guru/taxi driver, "Be sure to get in before 4 o'clock or it will close." Yes, go ahead and say it—we were forbidden from the Forbidden City. But we thought we were in! It sure looked right. We show our friends the pictures, and they don't know the difference (because we don't tell them). We got distracted on the journey and didn't make it to our destination. In fact, we never experienced the best part of the journey because we settled for the outer courts.

Have you ever wondered if there was more to the Christian life than what you see? *"It doesn't get any better than this"*—or does it? Do you feel like most of the Christians around you have settled for a smaller existence than what the men and women in the Bible seemed to live? I feel like that. I always wanted my life to count. I wanted to live for something that was going to last. Like kids who will sneak out and write their names in the wet concrete—we desire to leave our mark on the world. The scariest thing for this generation is that their lives may turn out like movies we watch where everyone works in some little cubicle, hates their job, and finds little meaning or joy to their life. Is that the fate of every person—Dilbert? A moment that captures this fear well is in the movie "City Slickers" when Billy Crystal realizes that he sells advertising time on the radio. *"What do I have to show for my life, I sell air!"* Over the past few years as I travel and connect with college students and Christians all over the country, I have begun to realize one thing. They want a purpose to live for. I know it when I see it because it's the same desire that has resonates from my heart. For most however, there seems to be something that remains veiled about God's clear purpose for our lives. Maybe you're seeking the same answers and asking the same questions as others. Why does God even have Christians on planet earth right now? Why are you here? My friends and I used to joke around, wondering why our pastor didn't just baptize people, hold them under, and send them to Heaven right then. How do some Christians seem to rise above the normal Sunday–morning–attendees and live with this kind of passion and a vision? Compared to them, we sometimes feel like we are outside and can't find the door. Many around us seem to have simply given up and settled for life in the outer court. God has placed you here, even in this time in history, with a purpose. God has put you here, and called you to a relationship with Him, because He chose to use you in an important role in His story.

This generation is on an aggressive search for purpose. It's true that the world is running from God. Could it also be just as true that they are running to find purpose and meaning, but they aren't finding it in the church? It's a tragedy that the anthem that best describes our culture, "*I still haven't found what I'm looking for*," could come from children of the church like Bono from U2. The church has crucified risk and danger and cause–centered living and traded it for Ned Flanders—a nice, moral, safe, harmless religious person. No one is "looking for" that. Life is too short to be harmless! The Bible describes life as a mist, a breath, like grass that withers quickly and in a moment is gone. This generation sees the moment and desires to live it with a world–changing passion. They have gotten the message that life is precious and meant for a purpose, but the great fear is—will I pick the *right* passion?

pieces of the puzzle

"*Most believers die with an unsung song in their heart.*"

– Howard Hendricks

Each of our lives is like a unique puzzle piece. You were born into an old, boring, black and white picture. When you became a Christian, God plucked you out of that kingdom of darkness to bring you to the kingdom of His Son. He made your puzzle piece into a new creation. God shaped and painted you a beautiful, new design and color, with a specific place in mind for you to fit. You are now a color piece made for a new, full–color picture. *"For we are His workmanship, created in Christ Jesus for good works, which God prepared beforehand so that we would walk in them" (Ephesians 2:10)*. Paul used the word pioema—a word that can mean God's "workmanship," or even God's "work of art." You were created to be a small part in the masterpiece mosaic of God. We have a specific place in the big picture of His kingdom work, a destiny that we were meant to fill. The Christian life is the story of a journey. We are travelers on a road that has a beginning and a destination. The journey wasn't created for you; you were created for the journey. That is where you fit. God formed you and blessed you so that you could live to use your talents, skills, abilities, and resources on the tracks of where He is heading. Only when we see all that God is doing, and place our lives obediently into submission to the cause, do we begin to find the most delight in who we are created to be. We can be ourselves: a unique, colorful, and specially designed piece. We fit.

The reason why even Christians are still searching for purpose is that they try to take their new full–color puzzle piece and cram it back into their old black and white picture. They want to be a Christian and a new creation, but they want to hang onto their old plans as well. Maybe I can just be a "Christian" pro athlete, is what I said to myself. For others maybe it is becoming a "Christian" business man, or a "Christian" actor. As if it's okay to just put on a Christian t–shirt and keep on living out your own dreams. That kind of life will never lead to true happiness because it is centered on us. It is working from our plans out to God's, and then asking Him to join us, instead of asking Him what he is doing and what we can do to join Him. God isn't interested in joining your journey. You were created for His.

Sometimes people live in a state of hesitation, based on God's silence on the details. It's as if He is this travel agent who is planning your vacation. You expect all the details, no risks, an up–front guarantee and a money back policy if anything doesn't go as planned. Imagine if your travel agent just said, "I'm sending you somewhere, you'll see when you get there … can't exactly tell you how you will be getting there, just wing it and enjoy the adventure." Not our idea of fun. But neither is sitting at home. Don't be afraid of the unknown on the journey; be afraid of missing the life God has appointed you to live.

Before we can begin looking into God's purpose for our lives we must stop and ask some tough questions. If God were to reveal what He wants us to do, very specifically, would we want to do it? Are you sure that you really want to know? It is one thing to sit around and say, "Well God hasn't given me a peace about that," or "I'm not sure what His will for my life is." But it's totally different to know very clearly what it is that He requires of you and face the option of choosing His will or your own. Ignorance can be bliss for a season, but in the end of life, it is torment. The people that God reveals Himself to have no such hiding place. What God calls a blessing some would receive as a curse—because it's an interruption to their life and their agenda.

Before you can know what God's will is for your life, you must know what God's will is. You must have a God–centered, North Star for your life. What "picture" is God putting together? God is on a mission to redeem people from all nations. In Revelation 7:9 we find people in Heaven from every tribe, tongue, nation and people worshipping before the throne. That "picture" is the completion of God's work from the very beginning. God has created us not only to have a purpose but to know it. I am going to compare

Revelation 7:9 to a *North Star* that guides us—it's the big picture work of God. Your new piece is made to fit in a unique destination in the completion of this new picture. Everyone has a different place where they "fit." The North Star, however, is the same for all believers. We all contribute to the big picture.

The *journey* is the process in history and in your life where God brings all the "pieces" together for the good of His final purpose. To make your life contribute to the big picture, you must take steps to adjust your piece until you find its place. Some of the answers to our questions about our purpose here are only answered on the journey, but He has given us all the direction we need to begin. We are called to follow Him and walk the path He has created for us. We cannot sit safely at the beginning and expect God to give us complete assurance of all the details before we are obedient and become a traveler. Only the traveler will get a "map," a more detailed revelation and direction. A *map* on the journey can be thought of as a career, vocation, or specific plan. It's a packaged way of doing life. You are told where the roads are and where they aren't. Sometimes God gives people very specific instructions (maps) on what they are to do, but this is rare. The world, however, is a map factory. It continually bombards us with plans for success, agendas, and a promised road to happiness. A map is not always bad, but in the journey God will often lead you where there are no roads. You can't entrust your life to maps. The only way to be sure of your course in life is to trust something greater than the maps—a compass.

A *compass* is something that gives you direction. It reminds you of where true north is—of the big picture. The compass helps you set the right course toward your role in God's masterpiece picture. The only way to find our destination in the big picture of what God is doing is to live our lives by the direction of the compass. The great thing is that every believer gets a compass: knowledge of the general overarching purposes of God. We can know the North Star and set the course of our lives by it. The compass points the right direction and helps us determine the wrong maps from the ones God has purposed for us. Take these analogies and tuck them away. We are going to see how God gave direction to men and women in history as they aligned their life with His North Star and as they made decisions using the compass. I spent thirteen years of my Christian life in the outer courts of what God was doing. I was moral, growing in holiness, sharing my faith, discipling others, but I was still missing out on the "inside" purpose of God. Once I discovered what God was doing, I had a North Star to live my life by.

I want to lay out the clear purposes of God. His plans include you, the church, and the world. Your search for purpose and for living out your role in the big picture is going to be compared to a journey. My hope is that you will be captured by the radiance of God's North Star and live your life by the compass of what He is doing. Your desire to make your life count and God's purpose for you are designed to work together for your joy and His glory. It is the purposes of God that take a journey through history, moving through people, flowing through the miracles, speaking in the promises, carrying with force and momentum all the works of God toward one defining end. If we know that end, we can navigate our lives by it securely. It will not fail. We can ride the wave of the ordained purpose of God. In it is our destiny. God's story is revealed in His word to us, but not the entire story. The rest is being written right now as you read this. It is not written on paper, but written into history by the lives of the heroes of the world Christian movement—men and women who are laying their lives down for the global purposes of God. God's story is being written, not thousands of years ago, but today. The pages and chapters of our generation have room for one more hero—you. You will write a chapter whether you like it or not. It will tell of who you really were in the scope of eternity. What will it say of your life? Make it count. In this world *"the powerful play goes on, and we may contribute a verse."* (*Dead Poets Society*)

CHAPTER TWO

Direction not Directions

"God gives people direction more than directions."

all directions

"The enemy of the best is often the good."

I'm a fairly logical person, a real black and white thinker. The most frustrating thing for me is making a decision that doesn't have an obvious wrong or right choice. Either both options seem good, or even worse, when both decisions lead to negative outcomes. I can usually weigh things out to find the lesser of two evils and the choice with the greatest benefits, but when it came to my life for God, I felt like there were no tangible factors. In the Old Testament, the priests were commissioned by God to teach the people how to distinguish between the "common and the holy" (Ezekiel 44:23). The Christian life is full of great Christian things to give your life to. It is almost like we just Christianize whatever we want to do and call it ministry. There is something that tells me it wouldn't have been enough for the disciples to just put an icthus on the back of their fishing boat, instead of dropping their nets and following Christ. It's not about changing vocations, but about changing our passions. The church has been "snow blinded" by its own ambitions and now is lost in a blizzard of good ideas. So now for people like me who want black and white, I would settle for some shades of gray. To be lost in a blizzard, having all your energy and equipment, but still unable to pick a direction, is the most paralyzing feeling in the world. That person would give anything for direction.

Young people have within themselves the relentless potential to become world changers, but all this ability and ambition is also paralyzing. They are so talented that there are limitless things that they could set out to do and be successful at. This generation's worst fear is that they will choose the wrong path and miss their destiny. Since they can do everything, nothing is supreme. Everything is within reach, so choosing to grab hold of one seems to be more like letting hundreds of other paths slip out of your fingers.

It is much like the way a lion is kept in control by a stool. The reason a lion trainer uses a stool is that when he holds it upside down and thrusts it at the lion, the lion tries to focus on all four legs at once. He can't do it and assumes he is outnumbered. Eventually, he will back himself into a corner, helpless against this harmless wooden stool; all because he can't get over the fact that it has to fight four legs at once. To try to fight every leg is, in the end, to fight none of them. You have to be convinced of what is supremely important to pick a direction with your life. When God, your family, your friends and you all seem to have equally good ideas for your future, it gets overwhelming. This is where most people go into default mode. At times, when picking a life pursuit, it is easier to just adopt the first great sounding plan that comes along, or what we have seen others around us do. The answer to the problem is to know what is truly supreme in life; to have a North Star passion.

John Piper put it like this, "You don't have to know a lot of things for your life to make a lasting difference in the world. But you do have to know the few great things that matter, and then be willing to live for them and die for them. The people that make a durable difference in the world are not the people who have mastered many things, but who have been mastered by a few great things. If you want your life to count, if you want the ripple effect of the pebbles you drop to become waves that reach the ends of the earth and roll on for centuries and into eternity, you don't have to have a high IQ or EQ; you don't have to have to have good looks or riches; you don't have to come from a fine family or a fine school. You have to know a few great, majestic, unchanging, obvious, simple, glorious things, and be set on fire by them."[1]

The way to know what the supreme purpose for your life should be is, in a way, to know what the supreme purpose for God's life is. If God has a purpose for all He does, and if He has created you within the design of a wise plan, then your life will find its best "fit" in that plan. True trust in the wisdom of the Creator is evidenced by a life yielded to the Creator's design for our lives.

bad directions

"Our culture will validate anything." – Brad Buser

We haven't purposefully surrounded ourselves with people that tell us what we want to hear, but they are there anyway. The great tragedy of the Church today is its abundance of "yes men." We are so affirming of others that no one has the boldness to tell anyone they are wasting their life on temporal things. One reason is that there is a shortage of people who have a good grasp on the eternal things and the platform from which to speak this to others. Another is our love affair with encouragement and our fear of rebuke, both of which are keys to healthy fellowship. Be careful who you get to counsel you on your decisions. Unfortunately, most people don't stop and involve others at all, but even those who do only surround themselves with people that will give approval of their decisions. It's good to surround yourself with people that are wired differently than you and have a passion for God in other areas than you—otherwise you have just shrunk the world down to yourself and your preferences. That is too small a world for anyone to live in.

Everyone has one friend that still isn't married and people are always trying to fix them up with someone. I have a close one. He has had at least one serious girlfriend every other year or so since college. Eventually, he would find something wrong with them or they would break up, and right afterward—you know what all his friends would do? "Oh, I'm so glad you guys broke up—she was totally wrong for you." What is that? Once, while driving around in my car, he told me, "I have realized that I have very few real friends. What kind of friend would let you almost marry the wrong girl, only to tell you after you broke up?" My friend is a great guy; he's just surrounded by approvers. Approvers look on and don't love people enough to tell them the truth. Their thought was, "As long as the girl he is dating isn't an axe–murderer—I'm not saying anything." My wife and I have a term for that kind of sin. We call it "holding the coats." Saul, the persecutor of the early church stood by "approving of" the death of Stephen and several Christians. You know what he was doing? Nothing. Just holding the coats, not really involved, but not really trying to stop it either. Later in life Paul repented of that sin, the sin of consciously approving the wrong decision. Beware: our Christian culture will validate anything—even the wrong life purpose.

We need direction. But more than that, we need the right direction. Have you every played a prank on someone that asked you directions, just to see how far off you could send them. (Not that I've ever done that …) Anyway, just because you have a direction doesn't mean it is the one that will lead you safely out of the blizzard. It may lead you off a cliff. If you stand still you die, if you have the wrong direction you die. In this journey you need to move, and you need to travel in the right direction. A pastor friend of mine told me, *"I'm just like Frodo Baggins—I'll take the ring, I just don't know the way. Lord, I'll do this ministry; I just need you to lead me in the direction."* Many of us have the desire to be on mission with God and follow him, but are waiting on the right direction.

redirection

"Leaders climb the tallest tree and yell down—'Wrong forest!'"

– John Maxwell

In the book The 21 Irrefutable Laws of Leadership, the fourth law of leadership is Navigation. Maxwell says, "Anyone can steer the ship, it takes a leader to chart the course."[2] Once we understand the course that God's heart is set on, we don't have to worry about our ability. We have within us incredible potential for God's kingdom. There are many people climbing the ladder of success and achieving great goals, but the ladder is against the wrong wall. Just because we have a direction doesn't mean it is from God.

It is a hard thing to change direction once we have gained momentum down a path. When God encounters us in the journey, it almost always calls for redirection. The wise men followed a star, then left town a different way. Abraham relocates from Haran. Jonah redirects to Nineveh (eventually). God reveals His agenda and His purpose. Then we have to decide whether to keep on doing what we are doing, or adjust, redirect our lives, and join Him. Many times God would even change the names of His people to mark the redirection in their lives as a result of their faith and adjusting to join Him. God invites us to a life of redirecting. Neil McClendon says that, *"Life's interruptions are God's invitations."* God is not rudely invading our personal plans. He is blessing us with the opportunity to align our lives with the eternal. Here is where we find our chance to make a lasting impact with our life. If we chose not to redirect, we miss out on the presence of God working in and through us. And we miss out on the opportunity to enter a new level of faithfulness, where God can reveal our next steps. We can labor on the journey, but if we find that we are in the wrong forest, we must redirect to the path of God's purpose. Only His path leads to the right destination and the meaning, purpose and fulfillment that we are searching for. God knows where we want to end up. He has created the path and us for the path. As we look at His story traced throughout the Bible, we will get the treetop view and see the maze, the dead ends, and the path of God's purposes. Are you willing to adjust and jump paths? God may be asking that of you as you see His purpose in a new way.

direction connection

The biblical way we get direction is seeing the end for which God is working in and through us, and how we can attach our lives to it. My life was greatly changed by a planning strategy that is called "Beginning with the End in Mind."[3] We must begin our life purpose journey with the right end in mind. The end is what guides us. It's the final drawing, the blueprint for all our labor. Once we have the end product fixed and settled in our mind, we can begin to make the smaller steps toward it. No one takes random cogs, pins, metal, and glass, throws them in a box, shakes it up and expects a watch to fall out. Life, like the watch, has an intelligent design and an original plan. Just because you read your Bible, go to church, throw in a college degree, achieve some impressive accomplishments and raise a good family and shake those all up in a long life, it doesn't mean that out falls a life that counted for the eternal. It is amazing though, what great accomplishments can be made when the end is defined. Men in history decided to tackle Mt. Everest, and found a way to make the climb to the top. Others set out to be the first to reach the north and south poles of the earth, and with their clear destination in sight, made the journey reality. Even the once crazy–sounding–idea of landing a human on the moon became reality because people caught a vision for the end goal, and had a passion to bridge the gap between impossible and the possible. God's purpose for our lives is drawn out in His word. Now we can work toward it purposefully and intentionally. I saw a great principle in beginning with the end in mind that was biblical and logical, from which I could draw direction for my Christian life. The North Star is crucial for our journey. Without it we flounder because we have no guiding purpose to labor toward. We are the God–ordained connection between God's dream and its reality. The journey of fulfilling God's purposes has a defining end. We must begin the journey of finding our purpose with His end in mind—the fulfillment of the Great Commission. We were created to walk the journey. Our lives are the privileged means to God's end purpose in the world.

en route

God gives people direction more than directions. He will not rob you of the faith building experience of obeying Him for what He says, not what you see. We cannot expect to get all the detailed instructions before we are willing to begin walking the path. The bible doesn't lay out a "map." It gives us a "compass." The answers for our individual lives come along the way. There was a reality television show called The Amazing Race where teams of people would race literally around the world using only the transportation they could negotiate and finding clues along the way to help them. At each destination, there were more clues to where they were headed next and how they could get there. But they were not left completely on their own, or it could have been a miserable show. They were coached every step of the way. In fact, every team made it to wherever the destination was; some just made it slower than others. Even though they had a good idea of where they were headed, they had no idea how they would survive the journey. They trusted the guides. The answers came along the way.

Henry Blackaby says, "*When God tells you to follow Him, He is not obligated to reveal your destination immediately.*"[4] The final destination of our labor for the building and completing of His worldwide kingdom, we can be sure of. The rest of the answers for our journey are waiting for us down the trail. They are only given to those who trust in the word of the guide and follow His revealed clues one step at a time. Only the traveler gets the in–depth maps from God. He may not give you the details until you move forward, but all believers can start with the compass, the overarching purpose of God for His glory. We find His compass in His revealed word. It reveals the clear and true north for us to live toward.

"God does not have to come and tell me what I must do for Him, He brings me into a relationship with Himself where I hear His call and understand what He wants me to do, and I do it out of sheer love to Him... When people say they have had a call to foreign service, or to any particular sphere of work, they mean that their relationship to God has enabled them to realize what they can do for God."

– Oswald Chambers

1. John Piper, "Boasting only in the Cross," given at Passion OneDay May 19th, 2000, transcript available at http://www.desiringgod.org/library/topics/christ/ boasting_cross.html .
2. John Maxwell, The 21 Irrefutable Laws of Leadership, Nelson Press, 1998, p33.
3. Steven R. Covey, The 7 Habits of Highly Effective People, Fireside, 1989, p95.
4. Henry Blackaby, On Mission with God, Broadman &Holman Pub–lishers, 2002, p36.

CHAPTER THREE

The Map Is a Trap

*"If you live without a vision of the glory of God filling the
whole earth, you are in danger of serving your own dreams
of greatness, as you wait to do the "next thing" that God tells
you. There are too many over–fed, under motivated Christians
hiding behind the excuse that God has not spoken to them.
They are waiting to hear voices or see dreams—all the while
living to make money, to provide for their future, to dress
well and have fun."*

– Floyd McClung[1]

road map

Growing up most of my friends were into football,
basketball, and the usual sports. Since I weighed about 90
pounds in high school, contact sports were not really my
thing. I got into freestyle BMX riding—the stuff you see on
the X–games. I started when I was 11 and turned pro during
college. Back then it wasn't as cool as it is now, and by the
time I write this it will probably be lame again. I traveled
with a few friends to contests all over the country. At each
contests, we would pick up a flyer with a map on the back
to the next one. One day we got a flyer from somewhere
about an X–games contest that was coming to Fort Hays,
Kansas. I'm from Oklahoma, so this was like our back yard.
We had home field advantage. It was our territory. We were
so stoked. We practiced like crazy. We cleaned up our bikes
and took the 7–hour road trip to Fort Hays, Kansas. We were

so excited by the time the trip came that we were hanging out the windows, blasting the radio, yelling at truckers, all the fun stuff you do on a road trip. Most importantly, we were following our map. Fort Hays, Kansas is not big (it is actually pretty hard to find) but we had a map right to the building where the contest would be held. We got there the night before the contest and crashed at a hotel. I didn't even really notice that I didn't see any other cars with bikes on them that evening.

The next morning we woke up without an alarm clock. The registration for the contest was supposed to start at 9:00 a.m. We were there at like 7:30, and looking through the glass doors like kids at the mall. I remember thinking, "Dude, we beat everybody here, even … the people that should be setting up right now. Hmm." About 10:30 rolled around and this security guard drove up and asked us what we were doing. I showed him my flyer, and respond, "We are here for the X–Games contest, sir." He looked at the map and back at me and responded, "Your map is wrong. They moved that thing to St. Louis about two months ago." Then, to add insult to it, he added, "By the time you make it there you won't even see the contest, let alone be in it. Ha, Ha." As he wadded up our map and threw it back at me, I realized that we had perfect directions, but the wrong destination. We drove 7 hours home in complete silence, feeling like total idiots. I tried to figure out what went wrong. If I would have looked at a magazine or anything I would have easily found out that they changed it, but I had one thing working against me. I trusted my map. I didn't even question it because all my friends seemed to be going the same place I was going—Fort Hays, Kansas.

My Christian life almost took the same wrong turn. I realized that I was getting some great maps for my life, but I was locked in on a wrong destination. I got on all the right tracks—college, degree, career, and I clung to them because I trusted the map. But I had planned my life around the things that God was silent about instead of what He was clear about in His word. I was on the wrong path, not because the path was bad, but because God had designed me for another greater journey. In my mind, to walk a "good" path, but not God's, was in the end a wasted life.

treasured map

Many of the students I talk to are clinging to old maps that they have for their lives. Hollywood, parents, and friends all provide more than enough great maps for success and happiness. Friendship with the world and its maps for our lives can be enemies of God's purpose on earth and for your own life. The maps of most are leading toward the destination of riches, security, fame, pleasure, status, and the praise of men. The status–quo of getting a job, getting married, having 2.5 kids, the picket fence, two cars, going to church on Sundays (maybe even Wednesday nights), being in a cell group—all of this is considered the normal Christian life in America. It is not bad, but it has little to do with the journey that God is laying out for us to join into.

For some, their map is even an old calling from God that they can't let go of. When you learn new facts about the world and new insight into how God is moving, you must be willing to hear new calling from God and let Him give you a new map. I used to want to be an astronaut when I was a kid. I was also an idiot when I was a kid and didn't know jack about life or God's word. People get trapped by their maps. When I started trying to invest money in long–term stocks, the one thing they drilled into me is that I had to keep it in there. No matter how much it drops and how much you lose, at the end of thirty years you will gain!

While that might be true in investing, I see many students trying to ride out their career pursuits that way. People begin to invest so much in the form of time and energy in their degrees, careers, advancements, and positions that there is no freedom to make a "full withdrawal." They are unable to redirect on the journey. They are trapped by their map. Sometimes in life, when you see that you are on the wrong path you must make a costly full withdrawal. To get the pearl of great price, you have to purchase the field. It will cost you something to jump paths. Not because it is a real loss, but because you have stored up treasure in the wrong place and you will have to leave it behind. But the gain outweighs the loss in the end, even if you lose everything, because on the journey your value system will change. Our treasures will change.

The reason we cling to our maps is the map is secure. To trust the compass is to navigate the unknown. There is much of the God's purpose that remains undone because of Christians who are clinging to old maps. For this journey, we must be willing to set down our maps and allow God the permission to give us a new one. We can have a great map, but if it is the wrong destination, we lose in the end.

reading a map

The idea of those who are "called" to ministry or missions is a category we have invented, not to explain their behavior, but to excuse ours.

The reason I didn't question my map to Ft. Hays had more to do with reading the people around me than reading the map. The reason we fail to question the maps for our lives is that all the Christians we know are headed the same direction. As we look around, the lifestyle and pursuits of the average Christian look extraordinarily similar to the lifestyle and pursuits of the average non–Christian. The decline of the influence of the church in America is not because the world has become more secular but because the church has. We have claimed to have a treasure in Heaven but chased after the same treasure as the world. Do we think that we are fooling them? This has damaging effects on our evangelism and paralyzing effects in our church. Why question the things you are giving your life to when all of the spiritual people you know are headed down the same wide path? Most don't question. When someone does make a radical commitment to join God in engaging the lost world, we say that they are "called" to ministry. In reality, the Bible only speaks of one calling—*kaleo*, the calling to salvation.[2] Lordship, ministry, evangelism and missions are not electives for the Christian life. They come with the job description. Ministry is the business of every believer. We are a kingdom of priests (Revelation 1:6, 1 Peter 2:9), new creations and God's ambassadors (2 Corinthians 5:20). The idea of those who are "called" to ministry or missions is a category we have made up, not to explain their behavior, but to excuse ours. This idea attempts to justify the validity of a Christian who somehow doesn't do any of the things that Christ did or commanded us to do. Do not gauge your map by those around you. Comparing yourself with others does not lead to the direction of God. Comparing your life to the heart of God and His purpose in His word is the only way to get the right direction. We can only find those who are on the right path by walking down it ourselves and looking to see who is still around.

mapquest

A map is very appealing to a person looking for direction. However the map is an easy way out. It appeals to the lazy; people who desire to have the answers handed to them, and avoid the trials of the journey. I was one of those people, more out of fear than laziness—fear of failure. It seemed like I was just playing the good odds in life. My mind said, "Successful, happy people go to college, get a degree in this, live this kind of life, and plan this kind of future. Don't rock the boat, Claude. If this map is working for millions of other Christians, it has got to be fool proof. Stay in the pack so you don't get eaten." The map was just another security blanket for me to curl up with at night, so I could go to sleep telling myself I wouldn't waste my life if I didn't risk it. Beware of the mainstream pursuits of the crowds. You can take a canoe quickly down the river by staying in the mainstream, but by the time you see the waterfall, it's too late to get out of harm's way.

When I came to college, I was terrified about choosing a major. I had so much I wanted to live for, how would I pick one career, one degree. I admired my advisor and eventually asked, "Well, what did you major in? Psychology? Great, I'll do that." I basically closed my eyes and stabbed in the dark. What made the decision so easy was the fact that my advisor did something that appealed to my need for direction. He gave me a map. Take these core classes, a few electives, minor in speech, graduate in four years and destination success and happiness here we come. Easy! I could do that. My counselor had a great map, but he didn't know the compass. He didn't factor in the destination that I was created for: God's glory made known in all the earth. My quest and hunger for a map was so great that I almost forfeited my purpose to land in a place I couldn't get out of. I was on a wrong path. I didn't know it then, but later I would have to make a last minute jump.

Don't seek a map. Seek the compass. A map is no good in the blizzard of good ideas. There are endless maps to give your life to. There is only one compass and one North Star, one destination that matters. The great thing about a compass is it doesn't depend on you. It is grounded in something outside of yourself. The compass always yields to the gravitational pull of true north. A map is more detailed, which we like, but it isn't necessarily grounded in anything. It will do you no good unless you know which way it lays on the greater scale of north, south, east, and west. Seek the compass. The compass of God's purpose allows us to have something to gauge our maps by. We can check the map by the compass and see whether or not it is headed in the right direction. Our maps will change from season to season in our life, but the compass is unchanging. Its direction is sure. There will be seasons of life where you will be in college, a young single, newly married, starting a family, risking in a new business, maybe full–time ministry—but it isn't a vocation or season that is important. It is what you are living toward. The compass is the same for all men. It always gives the direction to true north, no matter what your language, your country, your social status, your family, or your ability. It exists as a firm standard. Seek the compass, check the maps.

1. Floyd McClung, *Apostolic Passion*, *The Perspectives on the World Christian Movement*, Paternoster Publishing, 1999, p185.
2. Rom. 1:6; 1 Cor. 1:2,9,26; Eph. 4:1; 2 Thess. 1:11; 1 Tim. 6:12; 2 Tim. 1:9; Heb. 3:1; 1 Peter 5:10; 2 Peter 1:10.

God's Purpose

"The story of God accomplishing His mission is the plot of the entire Bible. God's mission is the backbone upon which the Bible is built and is best understood. Therefore, God's mission is the reason there is a Bible at all."

— Steve Hawthorne

CHAPTER FOUR

Lift the Thread

God has one mission—all nations, and one method—all believers.

one way street

The Bible is one book. To see the journey in the Bible of God's purpose from beginning to end you must begin to see the one theme that is woven throughout it. I used to think that the Bible was 66 individual books, with common ideas, and written by people who had a common belief. But they seemed more like Aesop's Fables, with no theme, and no central purpose going on, just nice stories with simple life lessons to learn from each one. The Old Testament seemed old. The New Testament must be for me because it was new. I read Proverbs for wisdom, Psalms for worship and Revelation just for the weirdness. The stories of the Bible were like pearls, priceless in themselves. This is the Bible of the outer court. I was missing the big picture; the central story. When we lift out the thread of God's North Star in scripture we will see that the pearls are connected like one necklace, with a familiar, important, God–designed purpose strung through each one.

We are all looking for a story like that—a story that is big enough to live in. That's why people love *The Lord of the Rings* and *The Chronicles of Narnia*. Personally, I love the *Star Wars* movies. Rebecca had never seen one when we met, now, thanks to me, she is totally into them. We saw one on our honeymoon. Growing up in the 80's, everybody my age loved Star Wars. It was a cool adventure, I knew the characters, and I liked the plot. With each movie I was more and more drawn into the overall universe of it. It was a hit with everybody I knew. Then, in the 90's, when they began to tell the legend of all that took place before the three I knew, I found out that we had gotten ripped off. My generation only knew half the saga! I loved the story before I really knew it all, but now I really saw it. There was a theme that I had missed. And the character I thought was just a secondary bad guy, Darth Vader (Anakin), was actually the character that the entire series was centered around.

The story of what God is doing blows all the others away. It makes *Lord of the Rings* look like a pop–up book. It makes *Harry Potter* look like the funnies section in the newspaper. It makes the *Left Behind* series look like … the *Left Behind* series. There is a back–story to the Bible that must be seen to appreciate all that God is doing. There is a theme, another set of characters—the nations—that are more central than I used to think. That's what makes the Bible become a journal of daring adventure. There is a drama being played out and a war being waged between good and evil. Only from the view of the whole story can we see how central the purposes of God are in all He does.

step backward

When I was in Switzerland, I visited several art galleries. They had on display a number of famous paintings by

Van Gogh and Monet. I remember that one Claude Monet painting was over twenty feet wide and ten feet tall. It was one of those water lily pictures that are kind of hard to make out anyway. I could get close enough to see the texture and cracking in the thick oil paint, but I was missing the real picture. The only way to really appreciate it was by standing at the other side of the large room and taking the whole thing in. In order to see the big picture of God's story we must step back and look at the wide angle view of His purposes throughout history. To really take in the heart of God, we must step back from the 66 books and get the panoramic look at the big picture of His story. We don't just see a theme or an interesting observation, but the "inner court" of what God is doing. We see His heart.

the panoramic view

To help you get your hands around the idea, let me give you a short summary of God's purposes on the earth through His word. Let's lift out the thread and see the whole necklace, then we will look more in–depth at how each of the pearls are joined to the unity of the story.

The story of the Bible is a story of God's plan to gather the worship of all the nations that He has created.

Psalm 86:9 says, *"All nations whom You have made shall come and worship before You, O Lord, and they shall glorify Your name."* He has created man to fill the earth with His praise and the knowledge of His glory. World missions exists to bring the fame of God to all the peoples of the earth. It is about an absence of worship among people that were created to worship God. Missions is for God and His deserved praise. It is not merely to save people from Hell, or to help the less fortunate like some philanthropy that we add on in our free time. It is central.

God's global plan begins with a promise to Abraham that all the nations of the earth would be blessed through him and his family.

Now the Lord said to Abram, *"Go forth from your country, and from your relatives and from your father's house, to the land which I will show you; and I will make you a great nation, and I will bless you, and make your name great; and so you shall be a blessing; and I will bless those who bless you, and the one who curses you I will curse. And in you all the families of the earth will be blessed"* (Genesis 12:1–3).

God blessed Abraham with the gospel so that he and his family may be a blessing. God promises that this blessing of the gospel will make its way through this journey of his unfolding plan to a defined destination—not most or some, but *all* families (people groups or nations) of the earth.

God's purpose for Abraham's family was to be the pipeline that God would channel the blessing of the gospel through to all the nations He intended to redeem.

> *"God be gracious to us and bless us, and cause His face to shine upon us—Selah. That Your way may be known on the earth, Your salvation among all nations"* (Psalms 67:1–2).

The reason God blessed them was not just for them. He had the end goal in mind, reaching all the nations with the message of salvation. The reason God blesses us is so that we may be a blessing to the nations.

They were a missionary nation with a responsibility to pass the good news of salvation on to the ends of the earth.

Throughout the Old Testament, God uses the Psalms, the Major Prophets and Minor Prophets all to remind Israel that they were a missionary nation and a missionary family, created to worship and gather others into worship of the one true God. In Isaiah 49:6, God explains the full implications of the sacrifice of His servant Jesus saying, "It is too small a thing that You should be My servant to raise up the tribes of Jacob and to restore the preserved ones of Israel; I will also make you a light of the nations so that My salvation may reach to the end of the earth." In other words, it is too small a thing for this salvation to purchase only the Jewish people. God is too awesome for that. The responsibility for extending this salvation to "the ends of the earth" however fell squarely on the people of God. The church was the method. Israel, God's people, knew their responsibility toward the Gentiles, or other nations of the earth. The Great Commission given by Jesus to the disciples was nothing new, but was a continuation of the story of God's plan of world–wide redemption.

If you are a Christian you are adopted into this same missionary family and have the same responsibility toward the world that they had.

"Christ redeemed us from the curse of the Law ... in order that in Christ Jesus the blessing of Abraham might come to the Gentiles" (Galatians 3:13–14). By faith we become sons of Abraham and heirs of the promises of God. We are children of the same family, the family with a missionary purpose. In this family we are blessed with the gospel in order to be a blessing to the nations.

When we come to the end of the story we see that God has already pioneered the path before us. In Revelation we find Heaven praising Jesus because He purchased the nations. *"And they sang a new song, saying, 'Worthy are You to take the book and to break its seals; for You were slain, and purchased for God with Your blood men from every tribe and tongue and people and nation'" (Revelation 5:9)*. Now we must only follow Him and join in His work in making His kingdom come on earth as it is in Heaven. The church exists as God's ordained means of connecting the promise in the beginning with its fulfillment in the end.

Heaven will be a multicultural mosaic of all of God's created nations, languages and peoples gathered in worship, unified under the banner of the one true God for all eternity.

"After these things I looked, and behold, a great multitude which no one could count, from every nation and all tribes and peoples and tongues, standing before the throne and before the Lamb, clothed in white robes, and palm branches were in their hands" (Revelation 7:9). Missions cannot fail. God has promised to bless them through Abraham. He has already purchased people from every tribe and tongue at the cross. In this future scene in Heaven we find them worshipping as they were created to.

We can join God with full assurance that His mission and plan will not derail. That is why we can give our lives unreservedly toward it. This is the North Star of our journey. The compass of God's purpose points toward this one end. You may not have the detailed map yet, but in His word we can all find the compass. God has one mission—all nations, and one method—all believers.

CHAPTER FIVE

The first Step

*"It is a dangerous thing walking outside your front door.
If you don't watch your steps, there's no telling where your
feet may take you."*

— *Bilbo Baggins*[1]

put your foot down

You have probably heard the phrase that "the hardest
step in any journey is the first one." I'm not sure that's true
in life. I think the hardest step in any journey is not the first
one; it's the next one. We are on a journey where each step
that God directs us toward is going to seem to require greater
faith and sacrifice than the last one. Once we've begun, we
look back at the first step and laugh. It was hard then, but
it is never as difficult as the next step. We are going to see
that the people God uses in His journey are not people
who have incredible, unwavering faith; so much as they are
normal people that are willing to take the next step down
the path. God reveals the panoramic view of the journey,
the true north, but the path can only be seen one turn at
a time. Put feet on what you learn. As you learn about His
mission, your part, and the journey, the most important
thing you can do is take the next step.

the great divide

In the beginning of God's story there are two people, Adam and Eve. After giving them the Garden orientation and tour, God gives them a clear command, which is His designed purpose. *"God blessed them; and God said to them, 'Be fruitful and multiply, and fill the earth ... '"* (Genesis 1:28). God commands them to fill the earth with people that worship and honor Him. His desire is for a world–wide worshipping church. There it is, even from Genesis chapter one—the end goal. However, Adam and Eve sin, get kicked out of the garden, and fail to keep the Lord's command to fill the earth with worshippers. Two kingdoms begin to battle for the earth; the kingdom of darkness and the kingdom of God. Mankind continues to rebel against God until the flood, when God wipes mankind out except for one family of true worshippers.

When God floods the earth, He starts over with this God–fearing man, Noah. As soon as Noah steps off the Ark, here is what God says to him: *"And God blessed Noah and his sons and said to them, "Be fruitful and multiply, and fill the earth" (Genesis 9:1).* Sound familiar? It was the same command given to Adam and Eve to fill the earth with worshippers who honored and feared God. Remember, God's purpose for the world is not just to save the lost, but to fill the earth with the knowledge of His greatness and draw to Himself a worshipping church. He is advancing a kingdom, forcing back the kingdom of darkness. Noah continued worshipping, but his generation also failed to spread out and fill the earth. When we find them in Genesis 11, here is what the situation had spiraled down into.

"Now the whole earth used the same language and the same words. It came about as they journeyed east, that they found

a plain in the land of Shinar and settled there." (Notice that they still aren't obeying God's command to fill the earth. They settled in one place instead of spreading out.)

"*They said, 'Come, let us build for ourselves a city, and a tower whose top will reach into Heaven, and let us make for ourselves a name, otherwise we will be scattered abroad over the face of the whole earth.*'" Fill the earth? That was the last thing they were going to do. They were building a tower so they *wouldn't* be scattered. God, instead of getting angry and flicking them into the sun, does something very purposeful. This was all part of His design. God will divide and conquer. It says that the Lord confused, or changed their language into several languages and scattered them. "*So the Lord scattered them abroad from there over the face of the whole earth*" *(Genesis 11:1–8).*

All 12,000 ethnic groups of our planet today came from these first (seventy)[2] languages at the Tower of Babel. All the diversity and peoples and races of the earth are God's idea. They are His creation, and they bring Him increasing glory. Now the stage is set. The great drama has an introduction and will soon begin a plot. We have all the nations scattered to the corners of the earth, speaking many languages. How will God reach them all? God chose to begin one nation of His own. They would be His missionary nation and missionary family to reach all the others. Divide, then invade and conquer. One by one, He will win them and draw them back into a relationship through His Son. This missionary family begins through one father, Father Abraham.

"God divided the race for His purpose. He would reach them person by person, family by family, clan by clan, people by people, nation by nation. He then chose Abraham to begin a nation that would bless all the others." – Steve Hawthorne

leap of faith

Here is where the plot begins. The intro to the story gave us the background for the scattering of all the nations. Now God will create a nation of gatherers that will be His vessel for exporting the gospel to the ends of the earth. This is the first step in the journey of God's purposes. The rest of the theme of the Bible and our life purpose grows from the root of these three verses. The curtains open, all lights on center stage, and the new missionary nation of God begins through one man.

"Now the Lord said to Abram, 'Go forth from your country, and from your relatives and from your father's house, to the land which I will show you'" (Genesis 12:1).

Did you catch the first thing God says? "Go … to the land I will show you." What? Where's that land again? God doesn't give him a map. He gives him a compass. However, as He invites Abraham to join the journey, He reveals what the destination of the journey is all about.

"And I will make you a great nation, and I will bless you, and make your name great; and so you shall be a blessing; and I will bless those who bless you, and the one who curses you I will curse. And in you all the families of the earth will be blessed" (Genesis 12:2–3).

God promises to bless Abraham, but Abraham was not the final destination of the blessing. He was blessed so that through Him all families, or nations, on the earth would be blessed. This nation that God was creating and choosing had nothing to do with their uniqueness or with privilege over the others. They were created and chosen to serve. They were created to be the army that would push back the kingdom of darkness and establish the kingdom of God in every corner of the earth. His family was not the destination; they were just the pipeline that God was sending the gospel through on its way to the nations He had intended it for.

step aside

Do you know how a normal Christian becomes a hero of Christian history? They allow God to interrupt their life. Do you know where missionaries come from? They are normal people, who allow God to interrupt their lives. Do you know what the Lord is searching the earth for right now? It's a normal person who will allow the gospel to interrupt their life and their plans. When the gospel comes to Abraham, we learn two eternally significant observations about its authority and direction. The first observation you must embrace is that the gospel has the authority to interrupt the course of your life. God interrupts Abram's plans and separates him to make a nation of His own. God was blessing him and moving him into a position where he could best pass on the gospel to others. Imagine how hard it was for Abe. Packing up and leaving his family, his home town. He didn't even know exactly where to have his mail forwarded. *"By faith Abraham, when he was called, obeyed by going out to a place which he was to receive for an inheritance; and he went out, not knowing where he was going" (Hebrews 11:8).* He was the first to live life by the compass. There was no path for him to follow. When you are the first person to walk the journey, it's all pioneering. He had the faith to allow God to interrupt his journey, and by faith Abraham jumped paths. The reason salvation comes to you is not just for you alone; it is so that God may redirect you to a place where you can be a conduit of His salvation to others. God is blessing you with revelation into His plan and an invitation to join His journey, but it may require you to change directions and jump paths. You cannot walk both your journey and God's. There is only room in life for one journey.

As I finished my degree, I worked a little and realized that a Bachelors Degree in Psychology was not going to get me very far if I wanted the normal life. So I enrolled to begin my master's degree that fall. During the last years of college I was developing in my heart for the world through the guy that discipled me and through books I was reading. Meanwhile, I took the GRE and got the score I needed. I interviewed and was part of the twenty–five that were accepted into the program. It must be God's will right? There were two paths emerging in my journey; two maps for my life. However, I was about to stop living life by the maps and start living my life by the compass.

Literally a week before my classes started I did something pivotal for my journey. I went to a missions conference—by the way, don't ever do that if you want your life to remain uninterrupted. The speaker was talking about the history of missions and about heroes that I had never known. I remember him talking about the Moravians, who were missionaries a couple of hundred years ago that took the Great Commission so seriously that some of them sold themselves into slavery in order to reach the slaves. When they sailed to Africa they would pack their belongings in coffins, because they knew they would dead in two years from the diseases. And if that wasn't hardcore enough, he added this fact almost as an aside. When they got to the shores, they would unload their belongings, and then burn the ships right there at the shore. They had committed their lives and were not returning.

As I sat in that seat next to my wife Rebecca, it was as if God spoke very clearly to me about the two paths in my life. Claude, you have one foot on the shore, and one foot in the boat—just in case. One foot is in My plan and one foot in your little backup plan. Just in case my eternal reward is not true, you are planning on having your reward here. You can argue for the validity of your maps all day, but there is only one compass. The decision wasn't about whether or not I should get the degree, but it was about whether I was going to let the degree get me. Would I let the world's map hijack my blessings away from God's purposes and into some smaller ambition? I had been shown by God through the Moravians and others what it looked like to live life by the compass, and I realized that I had the wrong map. The next day I withdrew from my classes, quit my job and joined the ministry I am with today. The point was that since I was designed for this journey, the gospel had the authority to interrupt my life.

I often share my story with students because I think they can identify with the inner battle of choosing the right path. After one meeting a student came up to me and said that his worst fear was, to borrow my Moravian story, that he would get to the shore and burn the ships only to find out that it was the wrong island. I knew exactly what he meant. He was speaking my language, and expressing what is probably the great fear of most of this generation—to give their lives to the things that don't really matter. To redirect our lives into the journey that God has designed us for means that He must have the freedom to interrupt our plans. Even the map we have from God today must be reevaluated tomorrow against the compass. Every map has an expiration date. Our responsibility is to take the next step. The rest of the details come on the journey.

camera, action, lights

Henry Blackaby, in his book Experiencing God, makes this connection between God's revelation and our response. When God reveals to us what He is doing, it causes us to come to a crisis of belief where we have to decide whether or not to adjust our lives and join Him or to just keep doing what we are doing. Abraham heard God's voice telling him to go. He received insight into the future blessing that would have worldwide impact, but the revelation called for him to change his plans and join God in the journey. The place where God was going to send him would be seen later. Abraham had to obey to get the rest of the details. Instead of lights, camera, action as in filming a movie, it's camera, action, lights. We see through the camera lens of God's purposes, a revelation into what He is doing, we put action to it in obedience and faith, and then afterward, more light is given to illumine our path further. It's like that scene from *Indiana Jones and the Last Crusade* where he must take the leap of faith. Indiana is standing at the edge of a cliff, staring down at this bottomless chasm between him and the entrance on the other side of the huge gap. It is impossible to jump, there are Nazis behind him, he has no whip, there's no way! Then he remembers the faithful instructions of his father. He takes a moment to muster up his faith. Then he does the impossible: he steps off the cliff. Just when we expect to see him fall, our hero lands awkwardly on the unseen bridge a few feet below him. This may be how you feel. You would love to get to the treasure awaiting you at the path's end and be the hero that seizes the day, but the leap seems like too much to ask. The question is: Do you trust in the detailed instructions of the Father? Maybe they have never verbalized it this way, but many are living trapped by the fear that God cannot really be trusted to meet their needs.

Therefore, they resist the idea of surrendering their life to him completely. To surrender to God's purpose for you is not to plunge into death; it is to find the bridge to true life. Ultimately everyone surrenders to something. Either you will surrender to life in the outer courts, or you will surrender to God in faith, adjust your life in obedience, and find the life you were created to live.

get in step

The second observation that we must embrace is that the gospel of God is going somewhere. The gospel has a destination: all nations. God is gathering some from every tribe and people group on the earth. A good picture of the gathering of the nations is found in how God used Noah and the ark. God commanded Noah to gather some of every kind of animal and preserve them through the ark, so that they would survive the flood. This would preserve God's beautiful and diverse creation for the future generations to see. His creation is the display of His glory to all men. God is using another Noah–type figure, Israel, to gather not animals, but people from all the ethnic groups of the earth. This preserves His unique creation and diversity in the nations, languages, cultures and peoples that will one day display His glory to all in Heaven, for all eternity. Imagine if Noah would have only saved the elephants. Elephants are great, but there are an endless number of animals that God put on the earth as a reflection of His glory in creation, His creativity. Their diversity brings more glory to the Creator. There were some awesome elephants that died in the flood, because God was concerned with preserving some from all His diverse creation. The mission of God is not about saving as many people as we can. It is about gathering as many representatives as we can from every single people group on the planet. It is God's great scavenger hunt with a list of all the ethnic groups of the earth. *"My decision is to gather nations, to assemble kingdoms … For then I will give to the peoples purified lips, that all of them may call on the name of the Lord, to serve Him shoulder to shoulder. From beyond the rivers of Ethiopia My worshipers, My dispersed ones, will bring My offerings" (Zephaniah 3:8–10).* The gospel is to be extended through us to all the nations.

One of the most honoring traditions of the Olympics is the passing of the Olympic torch around the world by different runners. One runner will carry it a mile or two, and then pass it on to the next person, and to the next, until it makes its way across whole continents. Eventually, it arrives at the Olympic stadium and is used to light the Olympic flame that burns continually. The Greeks didn't run with a torch, but runners would herald the message of the times and locations of the games from city to city, proclaiming the invitation as they passed through. Today it is a huge privilege to get to run with the torch. Not many people have ever done it. They nominate you and you sign a bunch of waivers because there is an enormous respon-sibility that comes along with carrying the Olympic Torch. The main and most obvious responsibility is to pass it on. Can you imagine if some idiot tried to jump in his car and take the torch home as a souvenir? Every true–blooded American man, woman, child and senior citizen would be on a headhunt for this loser who ruined the Olympic tradition and embarrassed our country. As far as I know nobody has ever done that! You know why? Because of the weight of responsibility that comes along with carrying the torch. People ran with it before and people are waiting for it down the road.

This gospel that comes to us is no different. The gospel comes to you on its way to someone else. There are people who have carried it before you, and there are unreached peoples among the nations that are awaiting its arrival. The gospel comes to you on its way to people in your city and eventually to people in every nation. If you have been given the pass, you are a runner; there are no spectators. This race is not a solo sprint—it is a relay. The journey of the gospel has a clear and defined destination. It will be a part of a more lasting destination than the Olympic flame, because it is bringing into Heaven people from every nation gathered into worship of God for all eternity. This is the true north of our journey. Follow the compass and you will be a part of putting it together.

Just to make the North Star clear to Abraham, God makes two more promises to him concerning the nations. First, in Genesis 18:18 saying, *"Abraham will surely become a great and mighty nation, and in him all the nations of the earth will be blessed,"* and later after he was faithful in offering up Isaac as sacrifice, God swears by His own name that *"in your seed all the nations of the earth shall be blessed, because you have obeyed My voice"* (Genesis 22:18). God promises that this missionary nation will eventually gather people from, not most, or some, but ALL nations of the earth.

a family with a purpose

God is starting a missionary nation and a missionary family. The promise is that through Abraham's family line, Israel and the Jews (from which Jesus would come), that all the nations will be blessed. They are the children in step with the journey, set apart for the journey. God says that all nations will be blessed through Abraham and his family. It's a family thing. Here is what God says to Abraham's son, Isaac. *"I will multiply your descendants as the stars of Heaven, and will give your descendants all these lands; and by your descendants all the nations of the earth shall be blessed"* (Genesis 26:4). That is what it meant to be in this family. They carried the responsibility of blessing all the nations with salvation. Later God makes a similar promise to Isaac's son Jacob, saying, *"Your descendants will also be like the dust of the earth, and you will spread out to the west and to the east and to the north and to the south; and in you and in your descendants shall all the families of the earth be blessed"* (Genesis 28:14).

Imagine you dad sitting you down and telling you, "Welcome to the family my son. You are going to be blessed, but with the blessing comes great responsibility. All the nations of the earth are dependent on us to obey the Lord and the purpose for which He created us. We cannot horde the blessing to ourselves; we have been blessed to be a blessing."

The Israelites had a term for other nations, referring to them as Gentiles (that would be most of us). They used the word Gentile for anyone or any nation that was not Jewish. If a Gentile wanted to convert to Judaism, his salvation was still based on faith in the future messiah, but he would have to become circumcised and begin following the Old Testament Law.

Now the question is—how do you and I, Gentiles, fit into God's mission for Abraham and the nation of Israel? They are God's chosen people, not us. The answer is that it's a family thing; anyone in the family has the responsibility. This family grows not through physical birth, but through spiritual birth.

The great mystery of the New Testament is that through the cross, we Gentiles are now born into God's family by faith in Jesus. When that happens, we (Gentiles) are adopted into the family of Abraham and are considered sons (Galatians 3:7, 26; Romans 9:8). In other words, God's missionary family is an adopted army of people from every nation, created to gather every nation. If you are a Christian, you are in the family and responsible for the family mission—the salvation of all the nations.

stepping stones

"Therefore, be sure that it is those who are of faith who are sons of Abraham" (Galatians 3:7).

Try to read this with a fresh new Gentile perspective. Through Christ's work on the cross, providing salvation by faith alone, God is able to raise up true children from stones if He desires (Matthew 3:9). It is no longer the lineage that is important. It is the circumcision of the heart.

"Therefore remember that formerly you, the Gentiles in the flesh, who are called 'Uncircumcision' by the so-called 'Circumcision,' which is performed in the flesh by human hands—remember that you were at that time separate from Christ, excluded from the commonwealth of Israel, and strangers to the covenants of promise, having no hope and without God in the world. But now in Christ Jesus you who formerly were far off have been brought near by the blood of Christ. For He Himself is our peace, who made both groups into one and broke down the barrier of the dividing wall, by abolishing in His flesh the enmity, which is the Law of commandments contained in ordinances, so that in Himself He might make the two into one new man, thus establishing peace, and might reconcile them both in one body to God through the cross, by it having put to death the enmity. And He came and preached peace to you who were far away, and peace to those who were near; for through Him we both have our access in one Spirit to the Father. So then you are no longer strangers and aliens, but you are fellow citizens with the saints, and are of God's household" (Ephesians 2:11–19).

It is a family thing—Abraham, Isaac, Jacob, and now you. You have been grafted into this same family. If you are a follower of Christ then you are a son of Abraham by faith and adopted into this missionary family. You have inherited all the promises of God and the blessing of salvation, but guess what you also inherit when you get into this family—the responsibility that goes along with it. Welcome to the family, son. There are no civilians in this army. To be a part of the family is take part in the war. Don't get your cues from draft dodgers that may be around you. The gospel has the authority to interrupt your life, because you are now under the headship of a new family with a new Father. You were created for the journey that the gospel is taking to all nations, because He promised that they would be blessed through *you*.

---

1. J.R.R. Tolkien, *The Lord of the Rings: Fellowship of the Ring*, 2001.
2. In Genesis 10 there are seventy families listed in the genealogy that were scattered. Genesis 10:31–32 explains how the nations were scattered from these 70 families even though the story of the Tower of Babel follows in Ch. 11.

CHAPTER SIX

Momentum

All the stories of the Old Testament gravitate toward this one North Star—the evangelization of the world.

lift the thread

When God reveals what He is doing and how He has designed us for a part of His purposes in the world, we must adjust our lives so that it corresponds to what we know to be true. Like Copernicus and Galileo, we must live in the reality of the world we know. The less you know about the universe, the easier it is to believe that it revolves around you. With knowledge comes a demand for greater authenticity as we try to make our lives congruent with our understanding. There are some facts that will change you forever. You learn more than you want to know and are ruined for the normal life. Maybe we have settled for life in the outer court because we really believe, "It doesn't get any better than this!"

When we look through the rest of the Old Testament we see that all of these stories hang on a common thread through scripture, like the pearls on a necklace. All we have to do is lift the thread. Let's look at 10 pearls in the Old Testament and the thread of God's global plan as it unites each into the overall story: the Ten Commandments, the parting of the Red Sea, Solomon's wisdom, the Temple, David and Goliath, Shadrach, Meshach and Abednego, Daniel in the lions' den, the Psalms, Minor Prophets, Major Prophets, and then one negative example in the life of Jonah. Are you ready?

inward and outward

God's work in the Old Testament seems to be accomplishing two simple things for the reaching of the nations, one inward and one outward. God would work inwardly in the lives of His people, preparing them for the journey. He was making them more like Himself in character and holiness so that the nations would see a clear picture of godliness in them. He would also remind them of their world–focused responsibility through the prophets and the scriptures. God also would work outwardly, preparing the nations to hear by turning the soil ahead of the gospel and spreading the fame of His power through His miracles.

One basic thing that God used for His global purposes were the **Ten Commandments** which were given to Moses, twice, and a crucial part of our Old Testament. They were the guidelines for the lifestyle of the messengers of God. Here is what Moses says to the people after he has read the entire Law to them. *"See, I have taught you decrees and laws as the Lord my God commanded me, observe them carefully for this will show your wisdom and understanding to the nations, who will hear all these statutes and say, 'Surely this great nation is a wise and understanding people'"* (Deuteronomy 4:5–6). Moses told them to obey, because he assumed that the other nations would be watching. He knew that their lives would either validate or invalidate the gospel and the God that they claimed to serve.

How does this apply to us today? Let's say there is an international student who comes here from a Muslim country. For the first time in his life he gets to watch Christians, not what he has seen on TV, but real Christians with real Christian T-shirts and WWJD bracelets. (How else would you know for sure?) Then he sees what these same students do with their girlfriends, what they watch on TV, what the Christian girls wear, hears their language and watches their treatment of others, and eventually says, "No thanks, I'll stick with Allah. That's not a changed life or a testimony of anything." How many internationals live and work in our communities and rarely get invited to a Christian home, or even befriended by believers in their own communities? Our ideas of a multicultural church are far from the diversity of the church that God is building. God gave us the Ten Commandments to prepare us to be the echoes of His character before a watching world. The message is in the messenger. That's how God has designed it. God gave us the Ten Commandments so that we wouldn't profane His name in the sight of the nations that He is trying to reach. His Law is the preparation for the journey. If we are going to travel the journey, we will have to get in shape.

God had a purpose for the **parting of the Red Sea** that went beyond just rescuing Israel. He could have done that easily enough by leading them another way. Instead, God led them through the desert right to the middle of the Red Sea. The parting of the Red Sea and their rescue wasn't about their blessing alone. It was about the gospel and the fame of the Lord reaching the nations. The news of what happened spread to all the surrounding peoples. The gospel gets gossiped across the land from one traveler to the next, recounting the amazing story of the God of the Israelites. In the years afterward, when the spies went to scout out the land, they found refuge there with a prostitute named Rahab. Why didn't she turn them in? Why did she help them, knowing that they were later going to come and destroy her city? It's because she had heard of the power of their God and believed in Him enough to fear the Lord.

> *"Rahab said to the men, 'I know that the Lord has given you the land, and that the terror of you has fallen on us, and that all the inhabitants of the land have melted away before you. For <u>we have heard how the Lord dried up the water of the Red Sea</u> before you when you came out of Egypt, and what you did to the two kings of the Amorites who were beyond the Jordan, to Sihon and Og, whom you utterly destroyed'"* (Joshua 2:9–10).

God allows Israel to be taken captive as slaves into Egypt, but it is all a part of His missionary plan. He could have easily rescued them at any time. But God allows Israel to remain there for Egypt's sake and so that the nations will get to observe a "shock and awe" rescue. The Lord even tells Pharaoh ahead of time that he is just a tool in His plan. In Exodus 9:16 God basically explains that He could have wiped the Pharaoh out by now when He says, *"But, indeed, for this reason I have allowed you to remain, in order to show you My power and in order to proclaim My name through all the earth."* God was using the fame of His miracles to show He was supreme over each of the false gods of Egypt, and to draw out worshippers from all the nations that heard of His renown. When the Israelites finally left Egypt after the plagues, thousands of Egyptians punted their wooden idols and went out with them, leaving Egypt to follow and worship the God of Israel. The larger picture in all these stories is the panoramic view of how God is using them to make His name known "through all the earth."

God gave **Solomon** wisdom, but not just for Solomon's benefit. What would you do if you were the smartest person in the world? Would you assume that God gifted you so that you could make advancements in medicine, create new technology, write tons of books and win the Nobel Peace Prize? God's Design was to use Solomon to draw the nations to the true source of wisdom, Himself. The blessing still means interruption, even if it is moving up in life. God elevated Solomon with wisdom, so that He could move him into a new position to pass on the gospel to the nations.

"Men came from all peoples to hear the wisdom of Solomon, from all the kings of the earth who had heard of his wisdom" (1 Kings 4:34).

"Now when the queen of Sheba heard about the fame of Solomon concerning the name of the Lord, she came to test him with difficult questions" (1 Kings 10:1).

Solomon received the wisdom, but he also received the responsibility toward the nations. Solomon used the talent and intellect that God had given him with the North Star in view. God was later able to use Solomon to build **the temple** for the Lord. As he had moved forward in obedience and lived life by the compass, God gave him a map, a detailed mission of building the temple. Solomon knew that the nations would be drawn to it because of the fame of the Lord's glory. He knew it was the right map because it was in alignment with the North Star of God's heart—reaching the world. So when the temple is dedicated to the Lord, Solomon prays a prayer reflecting God's concern for the nations.

"Also concerning the foreigner who is not from Your people Israel, when he comes from a far country for Your great name's sake and Your mighty hand and Your outstretched arm, when they come and pray toward this house, then hear

from Heaven, from Your dwelling place, and do according to all for which the foreigner calls to You, <u>in order that all the peoples of the earth may know Your name, and fear You</u>" (2 Chronicles 6:32–33).

God uses unlikely people to make His power known on the earth. David was living life by the compass even as a young boy. When **Goliath** was standing before the armies of Israel and blaspheming the name of their God, he was taunting the Lord before the watching world. The armies of Israel were afraid, standing around with their hands in their pockets. Meanwhile, David decided that God would act for the sake of His name, so that it wouldn't be profaned in the sight of the nations. All God needed was someone who would go out in faith; a human altar for the fire of God's power to be displayed on. David knew the compass of God's heart and that God loves to act for the sake of His name. If you thought that the NBA had the corner market on trash talking, look at what this preteen said when he went out to fight Goliath.

"This day the Lord will deliver you up into my hands, and I will strike you down and remove your head from you. (That's the proper Christian way of saying I'm about to rip your head off.) *And I will give the dead bodies of the army of the Philistines this day to the birds of the sky and the wild beasts of the earth,* (whoa, that's just gross) *so that all the earth may know that there is a God in Israel"* (1 Samuel 17:46).

Can you imagine someone, like me for example, saying to Shaquille O'Neil—"Hey, I'm about to pop your head off and miss a few free–throws with it. Then when I'm done with you, I'm gonna feed the bodies of your friends to the birds." It would be a great enough story if I just *said* all that stuff—then got beat down. Unlike my story, the reason David made headlines is he actually backed it up when he defeated Goliath. The reason David went out to fight Goliath was because he knew the nations would hear about it. David allowed the gospel to interrupt his life and move him into a new position where God could bless the nations through him. God moved David toward risk and toward direct danger in the journey. These seem like the extreme examples, but there are actually only a few places in scripture where God interrupts someone's life and doesn't move them toward risk. Risk is normal. Danger is normal. However, the compass directs us toward the right kinds of risk and danger that honor God and work for His purposes. The confidence that David had in going out to fight Goliath was the assurance in the compass of God's heart; namely that His fame would be made known in all the earth. Risk for the North Star is in the end, no risk.

Surely not every Sunday school story from the Bible fits into this overarching theme of God gathering all the nations back to Himself. Otherwise you would have seen it by now. The reason we haven't seen the thread for ourselves is usually a matter of our man–centered approach to life—our amazing ability to see only what we get out of the stories instead of what God gets out of them. As we look closer at the stories of the Bible we see that there is not only blessing toward God's people, but another direction of blessing that extends to the nations. As we trace the journey through the Old Testament it is as though God has left us bread crumbs along the journey. With each story there are clues that remind us of the compass of His heart.

Shadrach, Meshach, and Abednego live for the glory of God in the sight of the watching nations. They defy the king, refuse to bow down to the false god of the king, and get thrown into the fiery furnace. Nevertheless, God comes through and they escape untoasted. Now, what usually happens here is this. We close the quarterly study guide and pray—all right, who's hungry for lunch? End of story. But wait a minute. Is that really all that happened? If you are still looking through the "me–centered lens" what do you see? Yup, I can apply that to my life. God will rescue me if I obey Him, or something along those lines. Wrong. God blesses Shadrach, Meshach, and Abed–nego, but that is not the extent of His concern. The story doesn't end there. Look what King Nebuchadnezzar does after he sees God act on their behalf.

> *"Nebuchadnezzar responded and said, 'Blessed be the God of Shadrach, Meshach and Abed–nego, <u>therefore I make a decree</u> that any <u>people, nation or tongue</u> that speaks anything offensive against the God of Shadrach, Meshach and Abed–nego shall be torn limb from limb and their houses reduced to a rubbish heap, inasmuch as there is no other god who is able to deliver in this way'"(Daniel 3:28–29).*

Whoa. That's what you call death–evangelism. This pagan king writes a decree, declaring that all these Gentiles (other nations, languages) must worship the God of Shadrach, Meshach and Abednego– the God of Israel. God gives Shadrach, Meshach and Abednego revelation into His North Star; they adjust their lives and obey Him. God moves them into a new position, involving risk and danger, so that He can bless the nations through them. Then God uses Nebuchadnezzar to send the gospel to the nations in the form of a letter. The blessing doesn't stop with our three heroes. It is just passing through their obedience on its way to God's destination: the nations hearing of the greatness of their God.

God does something similar in the story of **Daniel in the lions' den.** Daniel prays three times a day to the true

God even though there is a decree forbidding it. The king is forced to throw Daniel in the den with the lions for the entire night. In the morning, Daniel is just fine. But don't stop after Daniel gets out of the den without being eaten. There's more to the story than God blessing him. God is not through using the king in His world–wide plan.

> *"Then Darius the king <u>wrote to all the peoples, nations and men of every language who were living in all the land</u>: 'May your peace abound! I make a decree that in all the dominion of my kingdom <u>men are to fear and tremble before the God of Daniel</u>; for He is the living God and enduring forever, and His kingdom is one which will not be destroyed, and His dominion will be forever'" (Daniel 6:25–26).*

Again, God uses a pagan king to make His fame known to all the nations, peoples and languages. All because normal people allowed the gospel to interrupt their lives, even moving themselves toward risk and danger, so that God could bless the nations through them. Do you see what the compass of God's heart is directed toward? It is not centered on us, but it extends through us to all the peoples of the earth He has promised to bless. God may even ask you to move toward risk and toward danger for the sake of His mission. We are never promised that the journey will be safe, only that the North Star is reliable.

making melody

When David grew up he wrote the Psalms. They were songs that Israel would sing over and over. David was trying to remind them through the lyrics that they were a missionary nation with a responsibility to pass the blessing on to the ends of the earth. Just look at the direction of the compass as you see the emphasis given toward the nations in these Psalms.

"Ask of Me, and I will surely give the nations *as Your inheritance, and the very* ends of the earth *as Your possession"* (Psalms 2:8).

"Cease striving and know that I am God; I will be exalted among the nations, *I will be exalted* in the earth*" (Psalms 46:10).*

"God be gracious to us and bless us, and cause His face to shine upon us—Selah. That Your way may be known on the earth, Your salvation among all nations. Let the peoples praise You, O God; let all the peoples praise You. *Let the* nations *be glad and sing for joy; God blesses us,* that all the ends of the earth may fear Him*" (Psalms 67:1–4, 7).*

*"*All nations *whom You have made shall come and worship before You, O Lord, and they shall glorify Your name"* (Psalms 86:9).

"Tell of His glory among the nations, *His wonderful deeds* among all the peoples. *Ascribe to the Lord, O families of the peoples, ascribe to the Lord glory and strength. Ascribe to the Lord the glory of His name; bring an offering and come into His courts. Worship the Lord in holy attire; tremble before Him, all the earth. Say among the nations, the Lord reigns"* (Psalms 96:3, 7–10).

God's purpose for giving blessings is so that the blessings would be given toward God's purposes. Every God–given blessing has a Great Commission responsibility. The historical books of the Bible and their stories reflect God's agenda, and the poetical books like Psalms point the way to God's desire for the nations. When we check the **Major Prophets**, we can find that they also knew of God's promise. They knew the North Star that all of history was working toward.

"For the earth will be full of the knowledge of the Lord as the waters cover the sea" (Isaiah 11:9).

"And on this mountain He will swallow up the covering which is over all peoples, even the veil which is stretched over all nations" (Isaiah 25:7).

God tells Israel His purpose for them through the prophet Isaiah. It wasn't just about them. They weren't the destination; they were just the pipeline. The God of Israel was not just a tribal deity that was only concerned about the salvation of this one Jewish ethnic group of the world. He had created the nations and has created His people for the journey of taking the gospel to each one of them. This passage about the coming Servant of Yahweh, Jesus, is vital in New Testament understanding of Jesus' purchase at the cross and the implications of that for us.

"It is too small a thing that You should be My Servant to raise up the tribes of Jacob and to restore the preserved ones of Israel; I will also make You a light of the nations so that My salvation may reach to the end of the earth" (Isaiah 49:6).

God declares that the sacrifice of His son will not carry its full weight if it is only seen as a salvation for the Jews. The "tribes of Jacob" refers to their own nation, their own people – that's too small a purchase for price of the cross. However, what is implied for us is that the way in which this salvation is going to "reach to the end of the earth" is through our participation with Christ is spreading it through evangelism and missions. Paul takes this verse about Jesus and applies the responsibility of it directly to believers in *Acts 13:47, "For this is what the Lord has commanded us, 'I have placed you as a light for the Gentiles, that you may bring salvation to the end of the earth'".*

God had to keep reminding Israel, like us, that they were not to just be concerned with themselves and people like them. The extent of God's heart is for all the nations of the earth. If that is God's purpose, then anything short of that is too small. God is too awesome just to be the God of America, or Brazil, or China—He is the God of all the earth. There are no other gods besides Him, and He deserves the worship of all the nations.

The **Minor Prophets** also proclaim God's mission of world–wide redemption to the church. They were the voices guiding God's people and sometimes rebuking them for living only for themselves. The Minor Prophets were used by God to proclaim great missionary promises that we can anchor our lives on.

"For the earth will be filled with the knowledge of the glory of the Lord, as the waters cover the sea" (Habakkuk 2:14).

"'So many peoples and mighty nations will come to seek the Lord of hosts. In those days ten men from all the nations will grasp the garment of a Jew, saying, 'Let us go with you, for we have heard that God is with you'"(Zechariah 8:20–23).

detour

There are other examples that aren't so impressive. One is Jonah, who was sent by the Lord as a missionary to Nineveh. Instead of going, he rebelled and ran from his purpose. He knew the compass of God's heart. In fact, that was the reason Jonah didn't want to go. They were worse than just a rival country, they were the enemy. He hated those people. They had probably killed his relatives in the past, and Jonah knew that because of God's plan for the nations, He would be *"merciful and slow to anger, one who relents concerning calamity"* *(Exodus 34:6).* He didn't want Nineveh to repent because he wanted to see them get fried by the Lord. Basically, God had to make him go. Jonah reluctantly preaches his eight word sermon, and the whole city turns to the Lord. In the end Jonah is still sulking because of God's mercy on them. He was used by God to bring salvation the nations, but He didn't live his life by the compass. It is possible to do great things for God, even become a missionary, and never let your heart be captured by the North Star.

Those not captured by the journey and the North Star will avoid the situations that might take them down that path. It is "strategic avoidance." When I used to try to play basketball in the eighth grade, it was a miserable sight. I stunk. That was clear to everyone including me. Keep in mind, I was seriously 75 pounds, 5'1"; just a little scrawny punk sitting the bench. I enjoyed being on the team, though. I got to hang with my friends, have fun. But there was a fear that my skinny punk friends and I faced every time we had a game. You see, since the uniforms were meant for normal people, not squirts like us, we would fight over the (maybe) one pair of medium shorts that the team had. Even those were big. The rest of us got the dreaded larges. This means that the elastic waistband was about 6 inches too big for our waist. What do you do? You can't bring a belt. Suspenders? No, we would "french–roll" them across and over (like that would be less noticeable). Now here was the fear. We were on the team, and we practiced, but we *never* wanted to actually play in front of people, for instance, our whole school. It's a well known fact that size large gym shorts that are french–rolled don't stay on when you are running around on the court. Ever try to dribble and hold your shorts up at the same time? Not fun. So my scrawny friends and I would strategically position ourselves at the very end of the bench and lean back. Most importantly, we *never, ever,* wanted to make eye contact with the coach. That was the death blow.

I do the same thing in my church. When the end of the service comes, our pastor does what all small church pastors do, the closing prayer selection from the crowd. I don't know what other people do, because I've never looked around. That's too close to looking up. In the glance around the sanctuary, there may be some split–second eye contact with the pastor. I'm usually taking that opportunity to fidget in my pocket for an invisible something that is keeping me distracted. The point is that my eyes go down because I don't want to get called on to pray. It's silly. I speak in front of people all the time, but I know how to avoid it when I don't want to do. We all do. People isolate themselves from real contact from others in order to dodge responsibility in the Christian life. It is possible to position yourself in a way that you never get convicted of sin, never get isolated out to serve, and never get asked about your walk with the Lord.

You may think you are dodging God since He hasn't spoken to you audibly. Or you think that you are waiting on Him when in reality He is waiting on you. The reality is that He has spoken. If God has put you on the team, he expects you to get into the game. A person seeking after God's heart has nothing to fear in being selected to be on mission with Him in the world. The men and women of the Old Testament are normal people who allowed the gospel to interrupt their lives. They lived life by the compass.

CHAPTER SEVEN

The Road to Glory

*God is the one being in the universe for whom self–ex-
altation is the ultimately loving act. And the reason is easy
to see. The one and only Reality in the universe that can
fully and eternally satisfy the human heart is the glory of
God—the beauty of all that God is for us in Jesus. Therefore,
God would not be loving unless He upholds and displays and
magnifies that glory for our everlasting enjoyment. God is
passionately committed to His fame. God's ultimate goal is
that His name be known and praised by all the peoples of
the earth.*

– John Piper[1]

foot prints

In the journey, God leaves His footprints. When you
think footprints, don't think of that cheesy picture that they
sell in Christian bookstores, of Jesus walking next to you on
the beach in the sand. That looks more like some billboard
advertisement for an early retirement in Florida. I'm talking about big, monster, T–Rex type footprints. Remember
when the scientists in Jurassic Park came upon the T–Rex
footprint? There was a sense of fear and excitement and joy
and curiosity all at once. When God acts He carves His name
into history, leaving a deep impact that gives observers a
reverence for its Creator and an awe for its strength. That is

what it looks like to give something glory. We give glory to the creature behind the footprint and desire to know more. Anything that could make that kind of impact deserves to be known more fully. God commands us that whatever we do, we should do all for the glory of God (1 Corinthians 10:31). It's not that we can make Him more desirable, or more glorious, but that we would do everything in a way that gives full reflection to the true glory that God has. The reason we are to do all for the glory of God is God does all for the glory of God. His plan for the nations is that they would become loving worshippers of God, captured by His glory and in awe of His holiness. Throughout history God uses the reputation of His greatness as a trumpet, calling in the nations to Himself; a footprint, capturing our attention and leading the way to the Creator. The main way that the unreached see the glory and character of God is through the character of His people. God has made us to be the footprints of His name, displaying for the world that He can make a deep impact on our lives by turning us from the power of sin to the holiness of God. If people associate God's name with characteristics that are not godly, then God is misrepresented to the people He desires to redeem. Imagine if the scientist on Jurassic Park bent down, brushed back some leaves and pointed to a few bird scratchings and said, "There they are, the footprints of a T–Rex." First of all, the T–Rex would be poorly represented. Second of all, nobody would come to that park. There isn't the same sense of awe and glory behind the "puny T." If it seems important to represent an extinct animal correctly, how much more crucial is it that we represent the Creator of all things, the living and eternal God, correctly? God has an even greater concern for His name. It represents all that He is.

where the streets have a name

In Exodus, when Moses encountered God in the burning bush, God revealed to Moses something very important to God—His name. God was going to make Himself known to the world through Moses and the Israelites, but He had to make sure that when the nations heard about the stories, it was linked to the one and only God, not another false idol. That is one reason God would get so angry when His people were found to be keeping foreign idols. The danger was that the nations would become confused as to who the worker behind the miracles was. Can you imagine how tragic it would be if people, hundreds of years later, were trying to remember which god parted the Red Sea? God leaves no chance of that. When the Lord leaves His footprint in history He makes sure that everyone will know and remember who it was that acted. So God reveals to Moses a special description of who He is, referred to by some as His "fame name."

*"Then the Lord passed by in front of him and proclaimed, 'The Lord, the Lord God, **compassionate and gracious, slow to anger, and abounding in lovingkindness and truth**'"* (Exodus 34:6).

In the Psalms, David knows that God will link His fame name and His works so that the glory of His name will be made known to the world and remembered. That is why he connects them together in Psalms 111:4 saying, *"He has made His wonders to be remembered; The Lord is gracious and compassionate."* They are not two separate statements about God, but one. God will "make His wonders to be remembered" by using His fame name which is "the Lord is gracious and compassionate."

Later, when God was about to destroy the Israelites because of their sin, Moses remembers the description of God in His fame name: "being gracious and compassionate, slow to anger, abounding in love." Moses appeals to the Name.

*"Now if You slay this people as one man, then the nations who have heard of Your fame will say, 'Because the Lord could not bring this people into the land which He promised them by oath, therefore He slaughtered them in the wilderness.' But now, I pray, let the power of the Lord be great, just as You have declared, 'The Lord is **slow to anger and abundant in lovingkindness**, forgiving iniquity and transgression; but He will by no means clear the guilty, visiting the iniquity of the fathers on the children to the third and the fourth generations.' Pardon, I pray, the iniquity of this people according to the greatness of Your lovingkindness, just as You also have forgiven this people, from Egypt even until now. So the Lord said, 'I have pardoned them according to your word'"* (Numbers 14:15–20).

Isn't that crazy? Moses simply reminds God of who He is, that the nations are watching, and that they will think wrongly of God if He destroys Israel. He is almost using God's name as leverage to get Him to relent, and God loves it! God relents from judgment because Moses understood the concern God has for the fame of His name. You want to pray with power? Pray for things based on the sake of God's fame name throughout the world. God loves God–centered prayers. Others in the Bible knew the power of God's fame name and referred to Him by it during prayer and worship.

*"They refused to listen, and did not remember Your wondrous deeds … but You are a God of forgiveness, **gracious and compassionate, slow to anger and abounding in lovingkindness**"* (Nehemiah 9:17).

"But You, O Lord, are a God merciful and gracious, slow to anger and abundant in lovingkindness and truth" (Psalms 86:15).

"The Lord is compassionate and gracious, slow to anger and abounding in lovingkindness" (Psalms 103:8).

"The Lord is gracious and merciful; slow to anger and great in lovingkindness" (Psalms 145:8).

"And rend your heart and not your garments. Now return to the Lord your God, for He is gracious and compassionate, slow to anger, abounding in lovingkindness and relenting of evil" (Joel 2:13).

"He prayed to the Lord and said, "Please Lord, was not this what I said while I was still in my own country? Therefore in order to forestall this I fled to Tarshish, for I knew that You are a gracious and compassionate God, slow to anger and abundant in lovingkindness, and one who relents concerning calamity" (Jonah 4:2).

"The Lord is slow to anger and great in power, and the Lord will by no means leave the guilty unpunished" (Nahum 1:3).

In Ezekiel 36 we get a good look at God's concern for His name. Have you ever seen God get worried and show concern for something? God doesn't get caught off guard by anything that happens. So what would be so important that God would say He was concerned about it? It's the reputation of His name being disgraced by His people. God has scattered Israel among the nations as a judgment for their sin. Now He is going to gather them back, not because of anything they did, but because of the importance of His name.

"Also I scattered them among the nations and they were dispersed throughout the lands. According to their ways and their deeds I judged them. When they came to the nations where they went, they profaned My holy name, because it was said of them, 'These are the people of the Lord; yet they have come out of His land.' But I had concern for My holy name, which the house of Israel had profaned among the nations where they went. Therefore say to the house of Israel, 'Thus says the Lord God, It is not for your sake, O house of Israel, that I am about to act, but for My holy name, which you have profaned among the nations where you went. I will vindicate the holiness of My great name which has been profaned among the nations, which you have profaned in their midst. Then the nations will know that I am the Lord,' declares the Lord God,' when I prove Myself holy among you in their sight'" (Ezekiel 36:19–23).

God gets serious about people ruining the honor of His name. During college there was a fraternity that I had a ministry with, and I knew all the guys fairly well. I knew which ones claimed to be Christians and what they did on the weekends that sent a message otherwise. One day I think I'd had enough of God's name being profaned as I sat in the cafeteria with a table of "Christian" guys, one of which was bragging to a few girls about how drunk he was the night before. Right in the middle of one of his profanity–filled sentences, I turned directly to him and said with kind of a blunt obviousness to it, "I like your ring." I had noticed he had one of those James Avery icthus (the fish) rings. His eyes immediately fell to it and down as he tried not to make eye contact with me.

I pressed on, "What does it mean?"

The girl friends laughed and pegged it saying, "It means he can do whatever he wants on the weekend and confess it on Sunday."

I thought, "Ouch."

Then he, sheepishly and quieter now, says, "It uh … it means I'm a Christian."

"Really," I said, "Well man, I wouldn't tell anybody that." That may have been harsh, but the fact is that no one sins in a box. Our sin, mine included, effects not only those around us, but it stains the very name of God. Wouldn't it be better for the world (and the fraternity guys at Northeastern State) if people who profaned the name of Jesus with their lives didn't claim to be the examples of Christianity to the watching world? No wonder no one is running to the church. They don't see a difference in our lives. God will purify His Church through discipline, rebuke, the continuing work of sanctification and the power of the Holy Spirit to make us an honoring representative of His name. Would you think I was going too far if I said that God does *all things* for His name's sake? It refers to the "name" of the Lord over 100 times in the Psalms and 34 times in the book of Acts. God commands us to do all for the Glory of God, but does God also keep the command to do all for the Glory of God? Look at some of the examples from scripture of what God did for the sake of His name and His glory.

God created us for His name's sake

"Everyone who is called by My name, and whom I have created for My glory, whom I have formed, even whom I have made" (Isaiah 43:7).

Forgives our sin for His name's sake

"Help us, O God of our salvation, for the glory of Your name; and deliver us and forgive our sins for Your name's sake" (Psalms 79:9).

"I am writing to you, little children, because your sins have been forgiven you for His name's sake" (1 John 2:12).

"For Your name's sake, O Lord, pardon my iniquity, for it is great" (Psalms 25:11).

"I, even I, am the one who wipes out your transgressions for My own sake, and I will not remember your sins" (Isaiah 43:2).

"Although our iniquities testify against us, O Lord, act for Your name's sake! Truly our apostasies have been many, we have sinned against You" (Jeremiah 14:7).

Leads us and guides us for His name's sake

"For You are my rock and my fortress; for Your name's sake You will lead me and guide me" (Psalms 31:3).

"He restores my soul; He guides me in the paths of righteousness for His name's sake" (Psalms 23:3).

Deals kindly with us for His name's sake

"But You, O God, the Lord, deal kindly with me for Your name's sake; because Your lovingkindness is good, deliver me" (Psalms 109:21).

"For the sake of Your name, O Lord, revive me. In Your righteousness bring my soul out of trouble" (Psalms 143:11).

Answers prayer for His name's sake

"Also concerning the foreigner who is not from Your people Israel, when he comes from a far country for Your great name's sake and Your mighty hand and Your outstretched arm, when they come and pray toward this house then hear from Heaven, from Your dwelling place, and do according to all for which the foreigner calls to You, in order that all the peoples of the earth may know Your name, and fear You as do Your people Israel, and that they may know that this house which I have built is called by Your name" (2 Chronicles 6:32–33).

"If you abide in Me, and My words abide in you, ask whatever you wish, and it will be done for you. My Father is glorified by this" (John 15:7–8).

Remembers His covenant of grace for His name's sake

"Do not despise us, for Your own name's sake; do not disgrace the throne of Your glory; remember and do not annul Your covenant with us" (Jeremiah 14:21)

Judges for His name's sake

"And I will set My glory among the nations; and all the nations will see My judgment which I have executed and My hand which I have laid on them" (Ezekiel 39:21).

"'I will shake all the nations; and they will come with the wealth of all nations, and I will fill this house with glory,' says the Lord of hosts" (Haggai 2:7).

Shows mercy for His name's sake

"Then you will know that I am the Lord when I have dealt with you for My name's sake, not according to your evil ways or according to your corrupt deeds, O house of Israel," declares the Lord God" (Ezekiel 20:44).

Gives us the Holy Spirit for His name's sake and glory

"In Him, you also, after listening to the message of truth, the gospel of your salvation—having also believed, you were sealed in Him with the Holy Spirit of promise, who is given as a pledge of our inheritance, with a view to the redemption of God's own possession, to the praise of His glory" (Ephesians 1:13–14).

We labor with Him for His name's sake

"And everyone who has left houses or brothers or sisters or father or mother or children or farms for My name's sake, will receive many times as much, and will inherit eternal life" (Matthew 19:29).

"Indeed, while following the way of Your judgments, O Lord, we have waited for You eagerly; Your name, and Your renown, are the desire of our souls" (Isaiah 26:8).

We suffer with Him for His name's sake
"But before all these things, they will lay their hands on you and will persecute you, delivering you to the synagogues and prisons, bringing you before kings and governors for My name's sake" (Luke 21:12).

"For I will show him how much he must suffer for My name's sake" (Acts 9:16).

"But all these things they will do to you for My name's sake, because they do not know the One who sent Me" (John 15:21).

We persevere for His name's sake
"… and you have perseverance and have endured for My name's sake, and have not grown weary" (Revelation 2:3).

We do missions for His name's sake
"… through whom we have received grace and apostleship to bring about the obedience of faith among all the Gentiles for His name's sake" (Romans 1:5).

"Oh give thanks to the Lord, call upon His name; make known His deeds among the peoples. Sing to Him, sing praises to Him; speak of all His wonders. Glory in His holy name" (Psalms 105:1–3).

"'For from the rising of the sun even to its setting, My name will be great among the nations, and in every place incense is going to be offered to My name, and a grain offering that is pure; for My name will be great among the nations,' says the Lord of hosts" (Malachi 1:11).

This excerpt, taken from *Bethlehem Baptist Church's Driving Convictions for World Missions*, gives an excellent explanation of the relationship between the mission of the church and the fame of God's name.

In Romans 9:17, Paul says that God's goal in redeeming Israel is "that [his] name may be proclaimed in all the earth." In Isaiah 66:19, God promised that he would send messengers "to the coastlands afar off that have not heard my fame or seen my glory; and they shall declare my glory among the nations." We believe that the central command of world missions is Isaiah 12:4, "Make known his deeds among the peoples, proclaim that his name is exalted." The apostle Paul said that his ministry as a missionary was "to bring about the obedience of faith for the sake of [Christ's] name among all the nations" (Romans 1:5). The apostle John said that missionaries are those who "have set out for the sake of the name" (3 John 7). James, the Lord's brother, described missions as God's "visiting the nations to take out of them a people for his name" (Acts 15:14). Jesus described missionaries as those who "leave houses or brothers or sisters or father or mother or children or lands, for my name's sake" (Matthew 19:29).

God is gathering to Himself a world–wide worshipping church from all the nations. God does all, including world missions, for the glory of God—for His name. The establishing of the kingdom of God among the nations is the establishing of the fame of His name. As we spread the news of how awesome God is, the nations are drawn to the worship and enjoyment of God.

Two reasons why God does all these things for His name's sake: one, God does all for the glory of God, and two, God gets this glory through the fame of His name. The two are linked together. Now that you see the importance of God's name and His reputation in the world, you can understand how important it is for us to do all for His name and for His glory. His name is what links His actions back to Him. So when people remember His wonders, they attribute all the praise to the Lord and celebrate His worth. This is the worship that God desires, that all peoples would ascribe the proper "worth–ship", or glory back to Him. In the scripture, we see that the name of God is the vehicle that links the glory given by people to the true God.

God gets glory through His name

"Glory in His holy name; let the heart of those who seek the Lord be glad" (1 Chronicles 16:10).

"Ascribe to the Lord the glory due His name" (1 Chronicles 16:29, Psalms 29:2, Psalms 96:8, Psalms 66:2, Psalms 105:3).

"But You, O Lord, abide forever, and Your name to all generations" (Psalms 102:12).

"Now when the queen of Sheba heard about the fame of Solomon concerning the name of the Lord, she came to test him with difficult questions" (1 Kings 10:1).

They said to him, "Your servants have come from a very far country because of the fame of the Lord your God; for we have heard the report of Him and all that He did in Egypt" (Joshua 9:9).

"And blessed be His glorious name forever; and may the whole earth be filled with His glory" (Psalms 72:19).

"All nations whom You have made shall come and worship before You, O Lord, and they shall glorify Your name" (Psalms 86:9).

"I will give thanks to You, O Lord my God, with all my heart, and will glorify Your name forever" (Psalms 86:12).

"Not to us, O Lord, not to us, but to Your name give glory because of Your loving–kindness, because of Your truth" (Psalms 115:1).

"Let them praise the name of the Lord, for His name alone is exalted; His glory is above earth and Heaven" (Psalms 148:13).

"It will be to Me a name of joy, praise and glory before all the nations of the earth which will hear of all the good that I do for them" (Jeremiah 33:9).

(Jesus speaking) "Father, glorify Your name." Then a voice came out of Heaven: "I have both glorified it, and will glorify it again" (John 12:28).

"Who will not fear, O Lord, and glorify Your name? For You alone are holy; for all the nations will come and worship before You, for Your righteous acts have been revealed" (Revelation 15:4).

God is God–centered. God's mission is centered on God, not on man. Missions is about spreading the fame and glory of God to the earth, so that they may join in the joyful worship of their Creator. No one speaks more accurately and thoroughly on the relationship between missions and worship than John Piper, in his book *Let the Nations Be Glad.*

Missions is not the ultimate goal of the church. Worship is. Missions exists because worship doesn't. Worship is ultimate, not missions, because God is ultimate, not man. When this age is over, and the countless millions of the redeemed fall on their faces before the throne of God, missions will be no more. It is a temporary necessity. But worship abides forever. Worship, therefore, is the fuel and goal in missions. It's the goal of missions because in missions we simply aim to bring the nations into the white–hot enjoyment of God's glory. The goal of missions is the gladness of the peoples in the greatness of God

If the pursuit of God's glory is not ordered above the pursuit of man's good in the affections of the heart and the priorities of the church, man will not be well served and God will not be duly honored. I am not pleading for a diminishing of missions but for a magnifying of God. When the flame of worship burns with the heat of God's true worth, the light of missions will shine to the most remote peoples on earth.

Where passion for God is weak, zeal for missions will be weak. Churches that are not centered on the exaltation of the majesty and beauty of God will scarcely kindle a fervent desire to "declare his glory among the nations" (Psalm 96:3). Even outsiders feel the disparity between the boldness of our claim upon the nations and the blandness of our engagement with God.[2]

Although the North Star of everything God is doing on earth is the reaching of all the nations, this is not the ultimate end for which God has created man. Missions is only our *temporary purpose*, as Jesus said, *"We must work the works of Him who sent Me as long as it is day; night is coming when no one can work" (John 9:4)*. There is coming a day when our purpose in this life of reaching the nations will end. We can set the course of our lives by it for guiding our pursuit of meaning and purpose, but there is another, eternal purpose for our lives. Both of these are parallel tracks on the journey and both are working together. Our *eternal purpose* is to worship and bring glory to God. *"Everyone who is called by My name, and whom I have created for My glory, whom I have formed, even whom I have made" (Isaiah 43:7)*. The enjoyment and worship of God is what wells up in us and overflows into the world in the form of evangelism and missions. That is why Piper states, *"Where passion for God is weak, zeal for missions will be weak."* One way that we worship is to actively gather others into worship, to experience our joy together. God doesn't just want the nations—He wants their worship. In other words, the way to live your life for the eternal purpose of glorifying God is to align your life with the North Star, your temporary purpose. Those that are not on the journey cannot truly say that they are living for the glory of God.

a family for His name

"It is just as proper, maybe even more so, to say Christ's global cause has a Church as to say Christ's Church has a global cause."

– David Bryant

Israel was created as a missionary family to represent God. Their behavior and reputation would reflect God's character to the world. God now had his missionary nation that He would to stamp His name on. God wanted the earth to connect His name with the glory of His miracles, so He performed them through and for people that worshipped Him. He made them famous, so that they could, in turn, make God famous. They were a family for His name.

"He will set you high above all nations which He has made, for praise, fame, and honor; and that you shall be a consecrated people to the Lord your God, as He has spoken" (Deuteronomy 26:19).

"Then your fame went forth among the nations on account of your beauty, for it was perfect because of My splendor which I bestowed on you, declares the Lord God" (Ezekiel 16:14).

"The people whom I formed for Myself will declare My praise" (Isaiah 43:21).

"Behold, you will call a nation you do not know, and a nation which knows you not will run to you, because of the Lord your God, even the Holy One of Israel; for He has glorified you" (Isaiah 55:5).

"Then the fame of David went out into all the lands; and the Lord brought the fear of him on all the nations" (1 Chronicles 14:17).

"For Zion's sake I will not keep silent, and for Jerusalem's sake I will not keep quiet, until her righteousness goes forth like brightness, and her salvation like a torch that is burning" (Isaiah 62:1).

"The nations will see your righteousness, and all kings your glory; and you will be called by a new name which the mouth of the Lord will designate" (Isaiah 62:2).

When I used to ride bikes and compete in X–games contests, there were several companies that wanted me to wear or use their products. There was a shoe company that would give me tons of free stickers, t–shirts, and of course shoes. It was a matter of good advertising for them. We were the ones that would get our pictures in magazines or on videos. In fact every time their logo made it into a magazine, they would pay me money. I represented them. Younger riders see the pros wearing certain clothes or riding a certain type of bike and next think you know everyone's got it. All the professional athletes have sponsors that they represent: breakfast cereals, watches, clothes, soda drinks, cars. Where would Nike be without Jordan? The pros are given the goods because they are expected to display them. Imagine if you saw Michael wearing Reeboks in the NBA finals, or even better, penny–loafers with no socks like your dad wears. What would you think? First of all, every kid in America would probably be out trying to play basketball in penny–loafers that week, but Nike wouldn't be happy. In the book of Jeremiah, the Lord compares us, God's people, to a belt. *"For as a belt is bound around a man's waist, so I bound the whole house of Israel and the whole house of Judah to me, declares the Lord, to be my people for my renown and praise and honor" (Jeremiah 13:11).* Think of a prize belt for a heavy weight boxing championship. When the boxer lifts the belt into the air, no one is applauding the belt; they are applauding the owner and giving glory to the champion. God makes us a family for His name, but when He lifts us high the praise returns to Him. God chose humans to connect the glory to the name because we have the ability to *"declare His glory among the nations"* and point people to the champion.

When sponsors gave me these shoes, they expected me to wear them to contests, not just around my house. The gift demanded some responsibility to tell of and display the greatness of the maker. They wanted me to go out and represent them well. When an athlete starts to lose or does something to embarrass himself, it reflects badly on the companies he has associated himself with. God will judge and discipline those that bring dishonor to His name, not because sin hurts people, but because sin wages war against the glory of God. God does all things for His name and for His glory.

When Jesus rode into Jerusalem, He made his triumphal entry riding on a colt or a donkey, just as it was prophesied (Zechariah 9:9, Matthew 21:5). There is a joke about how the donkey believed, in his ignorance and pride, that the worship and cheering was all for him as he rides into the city. The truth is that the colt was just the vehicle God used to bring in the Savior. This generation is the colt that God wants to use to carry Jesus into every people group on the earth. The Christian life is not about us. The gospel is not only for us. He died not only for our sins but for but for the sins of the whole world (1 John 2:2). He chooses us to be the vehicle that spreads His fame into all the world. Along with the blessing of the gospel comes the responsibility to walk in a manner worthy of our calling. We live to the glory of God among the lost around us, and ultimately for His glory on the earth, so that *"the earth will be filled with the knowledge of the glory of the Lord, as the waters cover the sea" (Habakkuk 2:14).*

---

1. John Piper and Tom Steller, *Driving Convictions Behind World Missions at Bethlehem*, 1996.
2. John Piper, *Let the Nations Be Glad*, Baker Books, 1993, p11.

fork in the Road

"Christ redeemed us … in order that in Christ Jesus the blessing of Abraham might come to the Gentiles, so that we would receive the promise of the Spirit through faith."

– Galatians 3:14

changing lanes

There is about to be a seismic shift in the plot of the story. The torch had always been passed on to Jewish people, but the gospel wasn't making it to the nations. Israel wasn't passing the torch, they were dropping it. *"We were pregnant, we writhed in labor, we gave birth, as it seems, only to wind. We could not accomplish deliverance for the earth, nor were inhabitants of the world born"* (Isaiah 26:18). They were a missionary family, but they were not living life by the compass. They were religious, devout in worship, knowledgeable of the scriptures, but they chose not to allow God to interrupt their lives. Generally speaking, the order that the gospel followed, up until the New Testament, was from God to Israel, then to the Gentiles. It came to the nations more by default than by intent. It wasn't until the new Testament (Acts 10) that the church really began to take the gospel to the nations with intentionality.

Now the torch of the gospel is about to move a new
direction—sideways. God's purpose is for the responsibility
of the gospel to change lanes. Now the gospel will go from
God to the Gentiles, and they will become the carriers of
the gospel to the rest of the Gentiles.

> *"For this reason it is by faith, in order that it may be in ac-
> cordance with grace, so that the promise will be guaranteed
> to all the descendants, not only to those who are of the Law,
> but also to those who are of the faith of Abraham, who is the
> father of us all, as it is written, 'A father of many nations
> have I made you'"(Romans 4:16–17).*

> *"That is, it is not the children of the flesh who are children
> of God, but the children of the promise are regarded as de-
> scendants" (Romans 9:8).*

> *"For I do not want you, brethren, to be uninformed of this
> mystery—that a partial hardening has happened to Israel
> until the fullness of the Gentiles has come in" (Romans
> 11:25).*

> *"And if you belong to Christ, then you are Abraham's descen-
> dants, heirs according to promise" (Galatians 3:29).*

In the Old Testament, believers were saved by their faith
in the future work of the coming Messiah, and this faith
was evidenced by the keeping of the Jewish law. In a sense,
they left their culture and became Jewish. To make a com-
parison from the picture of Noah and the ark, imagine if all
the animals had to become elephants to make it on the ark.
There was a way for them to be saved, but their uniqueness
was lost, and God's creation wouldn't have been preserved.
Elephants are great, but God's creativity is not that impressive when the whole world is filled with just elephants.
However, God allowed all the animals to be gathered, not

for them alone, but for His glory. Even the animals entered the ark by faith, not by works. One way to think of it is that the Old Testament believer had to adopt a Jewish packaging. The inside was always faith in Christ, but after the cross the gospel could take on this new multicultural package. Now the Messiah would open the doorway of grace through faith, a doorway that anyone from any nation could pass through and keep their uniqueness. Otherwise, Heaven would not really be diverse. It would be made up of only Jewish circumcised nations that had left behind their former diversity. In this way, the nations will fill Heaven with their diversity intact, preserved for the glory of God and the joy of all nations. The missionary family of God is now adopting people by faith from any nation. They are sons, inheriting the blessing and the responsibility.

life of Christ

The prophetic promise to Abraham that all nations would be blessed through him and through his offspring is about to be partially fulfilled. "Through his family" was referring to the coming Messiah and also referring to the believers who would herald the good news of the Messiah to the rest of the nations. Jesus would provide the redemptive blessing for all the nations; the believers would provide opportunity for salvation by telling of Christ's work. Through both means, the work of the cross and the work of missions, all nations will be blessed "through" this family.

This missions theme of the Bible continues when we get to the New Testament and Christ enters humanity. As a baby, Jesus' parents bring him to the temple to dedicate him, and a man named Simeon takes Jesus and prophecies the Messiah's missionary purpose toward the Gentiles.

"... then he (Simeon) took Him into his arms, and blessed God, and said, 'Now Lord, You are releasing Your bond–servant to depart in peace, according to Your word; for my eyes have seen Your salvation, which You have prepared in the presence of all peoples, a Light of revelation to the Gentiles, and the glory of Your people Israel.' And His father and mother were amazed at the things which were being said about Him." (Luke 2:28–33).

Notice His parent's reaction; they were stunned. They had forgotten that they were part of a missionary nation.

Jesus' first sermon in Nazareth at the temple (Luke 4:16–30) was a hit with everyone at first. Things were going fine. Everyone was speaking well of Him. Then Jesus drops a theological bomb. He takes the promises that the Jews had always thought were just for them and interprets them toward the Gentiles. It was a *missions* sermon. How did they react? They weren't just stunned. They were so angry that they tried to throw Jesus over a cliff. Jesus was entering the world to rally His people back to their original purpose in life. They were created for the journey. He was reminding them of the North Star of God's purposes toward the world, even though it wasn't popular. Robert Coleman said, *"The days of His flesh were but the unfolding of time of the plan of God from the beginning. It was always before His mind. Everything He did was part of the whole pattern. Mark it well. Not for one moment did Jesus lose sight of His goal."*

Jesus modeled giving priority to the unreached early in His ministry, which is still an urgent priority for the church today. There were people in Capernaum that had enjoyed the benefits of Jesus' healings, but were unwilling to share Him with the rest of the world. They were like little kids that wanted to keep the whole bag of candy to themselves.

"When day came, Jesus left and went to a secluded place; and the crowds were searching for Him, and came to Him and

tried to keep Him from going away from them. But He said
to them, 'I must preach the kingdom of God to the other cities
also, for I was sent for this purpose'"(Luke 4:42–43).

Jesus knew that there were more needs in Capernaum, and there would always be needs in Capernaum. They wanted to keep Jesus right there with them, but Jesus had to move on to the unreached areas. There is a selfish side of Christianity. It is masked as love for Jesus, but really it is just a love for His gifts. True love for Jesus is to love the things that He loves—the world. They wanted the blessings, but at the expense of others who have never heard His name. Do you see this same desire to keep Jesus at home with us in the Church today? The friction against the purpose of God is surprisingly coming from the Christian culture itself. For every person I know who has made a move to embrace God's heart for the world and live their life by the compass, there are many more people in their lives discouraging them from their world vision. "There are plenty of needs here in our city." "America is the greatest mission field." "You're responsible to take care of your family first." Guilt and selfishness lead to manipulation and pressure to conform. The result is the same if we give in; Jesus doesn't make it to the other towns.

The living God is a missionary God. Jesus lived His life by the compass of what He saw the Father doing throughout history. He knew the North Star of God's promise to bless all the nations, and He aligned His life with the journey. Jesus allowed God to interrupt His life. That is what it means when we read in Philippians of the humility of Jesus and how he did not consider equality with God something to be "grasped" (Philippians 2:6). It is not that He didn't see Himself as equal to God. He *was* equal to God. The reason Jesus is a model of humility is that *even though* He was

God, He did not "grasp it." Jesus allowed God to make the ultimate interruption of His life (in Heaven) and move Him into a new position (on the earth) where he can pass the gospel on to the world.

Jesus continued to model for His disciples that God is the God of all peoples. Jesus did this by ministering to the ethnic minorities and Gentiles that were in the cities He went to. Several of His healing miracles in Matthew 15, Matthew 8:28 and Mark 5 were done toward Gentiles. The Centurion's servant that was healed was a Gentile (Matthew 8:5–11). The Samaritan woman at the well (John 4) was a Gentile. Jesus broke all the Christian taboos when He engaged in conversation with her. You know—the same rules that keep most Christians from having any contact with non–Christians at all. Jesus went to where the lost people were and was known as a friend of sinners (Matthew 11:19). He especially reached out to the internationals.

The purpose of God in reaching the nations and drawing them in was even made clear in the design of the temple. There was a courtyard called the "Court of the Gentiles." It was a special place for non–Jewish believers of the Old Testament to come and pray. Solomon referred to it when he dedicated the temple (2 Chronicles 6:32). It was God's open invitation to the throne of His grace, a place made especially for the nations that God loves and is passionately seeking. His purpose was to redeem them and He was sending a message that there is room in God's family for all the nations. That is why in Matthew 21:12–14, Jesus unloads on the merchants who have set up their gift shops in the court of the Gentiles. It wasn't so much an issue of them running their business in the church. It was that they had purposely set up their market in the area prepared for the nations. They didn't want the nations to mingle with them. As He overturns their tables, Jesus responds, *"My house will be a house of prayer for all nations."* The meaning is not that we should remember to say a little tag–on prayer for the nations after we've asked God to bless America. It means that the house is for all Gentiles to come and pray. Toward the end of Jesus' ministry the disciples ask Jesus when the end will come. Jesus knew that God had promised to reach all the nations. The end can't come and leave out a few or God will be made out to be a liar for all eternity. So, to help them see the theme of God's purpose for the nations, He answered the question by tying the beginning to the end. If you want to know when the end will come, you won't find the answers in the tabloids or in the end–times fiction books. Jesus told them, *"This gospel of the kingdom shall be preached in the whole world as a testimony to all the nations, and then the end will come"* (Matthew 24:14). If you want to live to speed His coming, live life toward the North Star.

It will happen. The reason you can live your life by the compass of what God is doing is that Jesus can never lie (Luke 21:33). His promises are sure. This is the end that all of history is moving toward. Everything in the Bible hangs on this thread through scripture: the fulfillment of His promise, the destination of our journey.

Jesus later summarizes the entire Old Testament and gives them the simple missions theme that runs through it. He lifts the thread out to show them the North Star of all that God is doing. They are blessed with the gospel so that it will pass through them to the ends of the earth.

Then He opened their minds to understand the Scriptures, and He said to them, "Thus it is written, that the Christ would suffer and rise again from the dead the third day, and that repentance for forgiveness of sins would be proclaimed in His name to all the nations, beginning from Jerusalem. You are witnesses of these things" (Luke 24:45–48).

Finally, in the last weeks of Jesus' ministry, He begins to more directly tell them their responsibility toward reaching the world. If they haven't put it all together by now, here are the no–brainers. As you read them, rise above the familiarity and attempt to see them in the broader context of all that God has promised to do in reaching the nations from the beginning. These are merely clear directions to the same North Star God has always had for His family.

"Go into all the world and preach the gospel to all creation" *(Mark 16:15).*

"Go therefore and make disciples of all the nations, baptizing them in the name of the Father and the Son and the Holy Spirit, teaching them to observe all that I commanded you; and lo, I am with you always, even to the end of the age" *(Matthew 28:19–20).*

"But you will receive power when the Holy Spirit has come upon you; and you shall be My witnesses both in Jerusalem, and in all Judea and Samaria, and even to the remotest part of the earth." *(Acts 1:8).*

God's invitation to live life on the journey is not a suggestion, it is a command. That is reason enough for us to obey and align our lives by the compass. The Great Commission given by Jesus was nothing new. It was a reminder of the original Great Commission that God gave to Abraham in Genesis 12. The commands of Jesus are not just last minute thoughts, or something to keep us occupied until He returns. They are the summary of all that He taught with His life and all that He saw in the overarching purposes of God from the beginning.

a road less traveled

When it comes to the life of Paul, it's encouraging to see that he was just a normal person who aligned his life with the bigger picture of God's global purpose. Paul allows Jesus to interrupt the course of His life in one of the most radical examples of change in scripture. Paul didn't just jump paths, he jumped sides. Formerly called Saul, he was a persecutor of the church, but the gospel interrupted the journey he was on. Even though he was religious, he moved toward counting it as loss. Even though he was respected, he accepted treatment as a criminal. Even though he was not persecuted, he moved toward suffering and persecution. Even though he was free, he became a slave to God and a prisoner most of his final years. Even though he was Saul, he became Paul and allowed God to give him a new purpose. From the beginning of his new life as a Christian, the Lord makes it clear to Paul what his missions purpose will be. *"But the Lord said to him, 'Go, for he is a chosen instrument of Mine, to bear My name before the Gentiles and kings and the sons of Israel'" (Acts 9:15).* Even though the Lord chooses Paul as a minister for the Gentiles, Paul assumes that the responsibility is for all believers. *"...Jesus Christ our Lord, through whom we have received grace and apostleship to bring about the obedience of faith among all the Gentiles for His name's sake (Rom 1:5)."* Christianity is about receiving grace and apostleship. Grace has to do with our salvation; apostleship has to do with the worlds. Salvation is not something to be received, but relayed. *"He Himself is the propitiation for our sins; and not for ours only, but also for those of the whole world (1 John 2:2)."* Paul was a logical person like me. He thought through things to their obvious conclusions. Just because God has ordained that His promise is to reach the nations, it doesn't mean that the *result* will happen apart from the ordained *means*. He asks these rhetorical questions in his letter to the Romans saying, "*Whoever will call on the name of the Lord will be saved. How then will they call on Him in whom they have not believed? How will they believe in Him whom they have not heard? And how will they hear without a preacher? How will they preach unless they are sent" (Romans 10:13–15)?* The answer in Paul's mind is that they won't. They won't call, they won't believe, they won't hear without a preacher—a missionary sent out by the church body. And the answer is not someone else—it's Paul. When God puts a need into your mind, that is His leading for you to be a part of the solution. Robert Speer would say, "*The knowledge of a need and the ability to meet that need—this constitutes a 'calling.'*" In other words, don't trust too much in a feeling. Paul may not have felt like he was the right person, or that he was especially called, but he took control of his destiny and willed obedience to what he knew needed to be done. He found a way to make the end goal, become reality. "*I make it my ambition to preach the gospel, where Christ was not already known, so that I would not be building on another man's foundation" (Romans 15:20).* Paul found a way to "make it" his ambition. If it was important to God, that was a big enough reason to make it important to Paul. Saul, on his way to Damascus, had become Paul who was now on his way to the nations. It was necessary in Paul's mind to continue to preach the gospel to the unreached where "Christ was not known." We will never reach the world by going to the same places over and over—the safe ones and the close ones. The only way to reach all the nations is by sending people to all the nations.

This is why a map for your life will never work. Remember, in the journey you can either choose a map or a compass. You can get a great map for your life from others, but a map will only take you the places other people have already been. The need in world evangelization is for people who will say with Paul that they are making it their ambition to preach the gospel where Christ is not known and pioneer to the unreached. Only the person that is living their life by the compass will make paths where there are none and pioneer new ones to the destination. All believers are expected, like Paul, to align their lives with God's global purpose and be a channel of the gospel to all the nations. When the torch comes to you, you become a runner in the race. God gives *us* the responsibility, because we are now a part of His missionary family. Look at the emphasis put on our role in the advancement gospel in this passage about becoming a believer. *"Therefore if anyone is in Christ, he is a new creature; the old things passed away; behold, new things have come. Now all these things are from God, who reconciled us to Himself through Christ and gave us the ministry of reconciliation, namely, that God was in Christ reconciling the world to Himself, not counting their trespasses against them, and He has committed to us the word of reconciliation. Therefore, we are ambassadors for Christ, as though God were making an appeal through us"* (2 Corinthians 5:19–20).

This is why you are a Christian today. The journey wasn't created for you; you were created and redeemed for the journey. God had a bigger purpose in mind in saving you than just rescuing you from Hell. He saved you to use you in His purpose in the journey from the beginning. *"Christ redeemed us … in order that in Christ Jesus the blessing of Abraham might come to the Gentiles, so that we would receive the promise of the Spirit through faith"* (Galatians 3:13–14). You are the great connection. This is where your life fits best, because this was the path you were created to walk. In your pursuit of purpose, without a vision of the North Star and your role in that, your life will remain disconnected from the original destiny you were created for. A train is meant to be on the tracks. Off the tracks it may not be in danger of hijacking, robbing, derailing, but it's headed for another danger—rust.

CHAPTER NINE

True North

His promise

All great stories have a great ending. All journeys lead to a destination. God's journey, His purpose to gather some from all nations back into worship, ends with a triumphal finale. This is the North Star that our journey is headed toward. One thing we have today that Abraham, David, Paul, and most of the heroes of the Bible didn't have is the end to God's story revealed to us in scripture. We may take this too lightly, without considering the fact that the great cloud of witnesses in Hebrews 11 joined God on His missions journey and allowed God to interrupt the course of their lives without these promises. Our confidence to join God in this journey is that it cannot fail. It is based on His promise, His purchase, and most importantly, His own glory. The mission of God to redeem people from every tribe and tongue and nation is anchored by the security of the massive promises of God. That is why we can live our lives radically by the compass of what He is doing. It is sure.

The journey is the only sure thing we can invest our life in because God has promised we will reach our destination. God promises that His mission will finish. The mission begins with a promise to Abraham, and it is sprinkled with other promises throughout the Bible.

"Cease striving and know that I am God; I will be exalted among the nations, I will be exalted in the earth" *(Psalms 46:10).*

"All the ends of the earth <u>will remember and turn to the Lord</u>, and all the families of the nations <u>will worship</u> before You" *(Psalms 22:27).*

"For the earth <u>will be full of the knowledge of the Lord</u> as the waters cover the sea" *(Isaiah 11:9).*

"For the earth will be filled with the knowledge of the glory of the Lord, as the waters cover the sea" *(Habakkuk 2:14).*

"This gospel of the kingdom <u>shall be preached in the whole world</u> as a testimony to all the nations, and then the end will come" *(Matthew 24:14).*

"<u>The nations will walk by its light</u>, and the kings of the earth <u>will bring their glory</u> into it. In the daytime (for there will be no night there) its gates will never be closed; and they <u>will bring the glory and the honor of the nations into it</u>" *(Revelation 21:24–26).*

There have been many places on the journey in my life where the hardest step was the next one. I remember making decisions that seemed crazy except for the fact that I knew they were decisions based on the compass of what God was doing. I would have waivered, hesitated or even turned back had it not been for the firm assurance in the promises of

God that this was not going to fail in the end. The promises are the markers on the journey that point the way, assuring us that we are on the right path. There are times when at the weakest point in my faith and the darkest part of the journey, it was as if the strong arm of the promises of God would rest over my shoulder and whisper, *"This is the way, walk in it"* *(Isaiah 30:20)*. His promises are sure.

His purchase

> *"And they sang a new song, saying, 'Worthy are You to take the book and to break its seals; for You were slain, and purchased for God with Your blood men from every tribe and tongue and people and nation'" (Revelation 5:9).*

The mission of God is anchored by the assurance that Jesus has already purchased the people from the nations we are to bring the gospel to. Jesus has sheep that are from another sheep pen, the other nations, and He tells us in John that he "must bring them." *"I have other sheep, which are not of this fold; I must bring them also, and they will hear My voice; and they will become one flock with one shepherd"* *(John 10:16)*.

We have the responsibility to take the gospel to the unreached, knowing that the Lord has people there that He has already died for and will draw to himself. My wife and I desire to work among an unreached people group someday. The hope that will carry us in the work on the field is that no matter what people group we land in, God has people there and He "must bring them." No one will ever go to an unreached people group and say that God has no sheep from that fold—our responsibility is to take the gospel to the people that He has purchased. Our lives are the gathering of the fruit of the cross; just as the first Moravian missionaries declared when they set sail for Africa, "May the Lamb receive the reward of His suffering."

His glory

God can swear by nothing higher than His name. Remember the great value that God places on the fame of His name and His reputation. His glory is in His name and God does all things for the glory of God. God will keep His promises, because first, He cannot lie, and second, His glory is at stake. God has put His glory on the line by swearing by His own name. *"By Myself I have sworn, declares the Lord, because you have done this thing and have not withheld your son, your only son, indeed I will greatly bless you ... In your seed all the nations of the earth shall be blessed, because you have obeyed My voice" (Genesis 22:16–18).*

God takes the keeping of His promise so seriously that He is recording the reaching of each of these people groups in a special book—the register of the peoples. *"I shall mention Rahab and Babylon among those who know Me ... The Lord will count when He registers the peoples, 'This one was born there'"(Psalms 87:4–6).* He promised to bless them all, He is keeping track of them, and He will redeem some from every nation. In fact, John records for us the conclusion of the story from eternity's view. In the end, before the throne there is a scene of the gathered worshippers.

the north star

"After these things I looked, and behold, <u>a great multitude which no one could count, from every nation and all tribes and peoples and tongues</u>, standing before the throne and before the Lamb, clothed in white robes, and palm branches were in their hands."– Revelation 7:9

To live life by the compass is to do all for the purpose of bringing this verse one step closer to becoming reality. It is to this end that we labor, for the piecing together of this picture, the North Star. Though we may perish on the journey, and seem to have lost in the short term view, the destination and the cause of God is ultimately furthered by our lives. The long term victory is sealed up in Heaven. What God promises to Abraham He fulfills through the church, the family of Abraham—just as He promised. Get used to the idea that Heaven will be an immense multicultural celebration! Maybe you will be in the minority for the first time. Maybe you assumed the official language of Heaven was going to be English, or at least King James. But it won't. It will be a symphony of peoples, making beautiful worship to the Lord. It will be a mosaic of different colors, languages, nations, peoples, worship styles, and all the diversity of the earth gathered and unified under the banner of the one true God for all eternity.

It is a triumphal ending. We must live our lives in the reality that the greater the participation, the greater the enjoyment at seeing its day will be for those who labored in faith on the journey. When I was younger, I used to travel on a team and compete in x–games contests. The guy who managed our team was somehow "in good" with the contest organizers. One time at a big contest, he somehow managed to slip away with some "extra trophies." He wanted to make sure we all went home with something. I'll never forget him holding them up and going, "OK, who wants second?" We all looked at each other and tried to act like we weren't totally embarrassed by his lame idea to divvy up trophies to a bunch of losers. If you've ever heard the word "poser" and didn't know what it meant—this is pretty much the best word picture you will ever have. How much more awkward is it going to be when millions of believers show up in Heaven, stand before the King of Kings and He says, "Enter into the eternal worship of all nations. You, however, had nothing to do with putting it together. In fact, as I recall, you never even shared your faith with those around you. Fortunately for the world, there were others who did—they made their lives count. This is their victory, enjoy the party anyway ... poser." What will the millions of sidelined Christians be thinking at the rejoicing in Heaven, over the victory in a battle that they never knew was being fought? Maybe the better question is—can the millions of Church–goers who never allowed the gospel to interrupt their lives really expect to be there? We must work, and live, and give, and risk, and die in such a way as to enjoy the triumph, not just observe it.

God is not wringing His hands in Heaven hoping that you will choose to live your life by the compass. You can walk the journey or waste your life in the outer court of what God is doing. His purpose will finish. We are privileged that God has invited us to be the means to the end. The only thing connecting the promise to Abraham in the beginning and its fulfillment in Revelation is our obedience to join God in His mission in the world. We see that the destination is sure, the promises are our fuel, and His purchase has paved the way. We only need to align our lives with the current of God's movement. We are the bridge between the beginning of God's story and the end. The conclusion of the story is written, but we must fill in the final chapters with the stories of our lives.

The Path Ahead

"God cannot lead you on the basis of facts that you do not know."

–David Bryant

CHAPTER TEN

Uncharted Land

"But I do not consider my life of any account as dear to myself, so that I may finish my course and the ministry which I received from the Lord Jesus, to testify solemnly of the gospel of the grace of God."

— Acts 20:24

road construction

This scene in Heaven that we have been talking about, of the countless millions worshipping from every tribe, tongue and nation, is an unfinished mosaic. It is missing thousands of "pieces" that we are responsible for gathering to finish this picture in Revelation 7:9. That is why the need of the hour is not just for missionaries. It is for people that would live their life missionally, committed with their resources, and for pioneers, committed to the unreached. First, we must know what the uncharted land on the journey looks like. Having traveled this far, we know that the destination is sure, but some of the path remains hidden, overgrown with weeds sown by the enemy, and must be cleared out for the gospel. Jesus has already pioneered the way, purchasing men at the cross from "every tribe and tongue and nation." (Revelation 5:9) The path is there, but it takes someone to obey and go the entire distance of the journey in faith. The only thing connecting the beginning of the journey with the end is people who will not look at the paths that have already been traveled, but will turn from the maps and follow the compass toward God's heart. There are no maps for the uncharted areas where the gospel has never been—it takes a person that will find a way: or, in this case—make one.

scout it out

In order to pioneer a new path, you must know the definition of where the journey is going and what remains to be done in world evangelization. If your pastor were to give a quiz on the number of languages without scripture, the number of unreached people groups, the population of the world, what percentage of the world has no access to the gospel and asked you to plot them on a world map—would you be in trouble? I want to help you get your hands around the basic facts about the current state of the world and the task remaining in world missions. I'm going to download some information to your mind. That way you will be able to make your life decisions with all the facts before you.

I am a fairly responsible person. I'd like to think I'm a finisher. When someone gives me a job to do, I like to be faithful with that responsibility and finish. The more important a person is who asks, the more responsibility we feel to rise to the occasion. If the President of the United States called and asked you to join him in a secret mission that would save millions of people from danger, you would feel a great weight of responsibility. You wouldn't have to check your calendar to see what else you had going on. You would jump at the chance because of the worthiness of the person that is asking and the impending danger to those who need your help. God is infinitely more worthy than any human in any position on the earth. If God has asked us and designed us to join Him in pushing back the kingdom of darkness and rescuing millions from eternal death; and if God has given us a task in history that moves toward this well–defined end, then we, by all our means, must be about one thing—the finishing of this mission.

A few years ago the movie version of *The Lord of the Rings* had just came out. I took a friend of mine to see the first movie in the three part series. You see the first movie, then wait a year for the next, then wait another year for the final one. Well, the only problem was I forgot to tell all of this to my friend. It's was three–hour movie and my friend and I were loving every minute of it. He was totally getting into the story of this fellowship–band commissioned to destroy the evil ring. During the three hours, he became completely wrapped up in the story and the characters as he watched them overcome peril, face danger at every turn; seeing some get injured, and some die on the journey. By the end of this emotional rollercoaster, when the movie just ends abruptly, he looked at me, back at the screen, and then punched me on the arm—hard. He was livid. He and I left the movie with a frustrated feeling (not to be confused with my sore arm). We had a feeling that something was left unfinished. My friend got mad because deep down he has the heart of a finisher.

God also has the heart of a finisher. The Bible is full of stories of other finishers. **God** finished the creation and rested on the seventh day (Genesis 2:2), **Adam** finished naming the animals (Genesis 2:20), **Noah** finished building the ark just in time to escape the flood (Genesis 6:22), **Solomon** was given the instructions for building the temple and finished (2 Chronicles 8:16), **Nehemiah** rebuilt the wall in 52 days, and the world was astonished at how quickly he finished (Nehemiah 6:15), **Jesus** finished the work of redemption, saying, *"I glorified You on the earth, having finished the work which You have given Me to do"* (John 17:4).

Now the Church has a task to finish. Not building temples, but building the church out of people from every nation and people group. That is why Paul says, *"I do not consider my life of any account as dear to myself, so that I may finish my course and the ministry which I received from the Lord Jesus, to testify solemnly of the gospel of the grace of God"* (Acts 20:24). In other words, he had found a cause to live for that was so profoundly satisfying that it was more valuable than life itself.

Is it possible that Jesus is saying to us what He said to the church in Sardis, *"Wake up, and strengthen the things that remain, which were about to die; for I have not found your deeds completed in the sight of My God"* (Revelation 3:2). God is looking for people that would have a holy frustration about their lives, a restlessness that would keep them up at night because His task goes unfinished. We have seen the first part of the story, but we must live with a deep longing to see the mission completed. This is what compels us to persevere on the journey.

the path of most resistance

The last leg of the journey may seem like the hardest. The area of the world with the greatest need for the gospel is known as the 10/40 Window. The definition below is taken from The Traveling Team website. If we are going to finish God's mission, this is where the vast majority of the work remains undone.

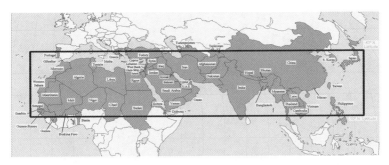

The **10/40 Window** is the area of the world between 10 and 40 degrees latitude, north of the equator in the Eastern Hemisphere, covering North Africa, the Middle East, and Asia. The window contains most of the world's areas of greatest physical and spiritual needs, most of the world's least reached peoples, and the most anti–Christian governments in the world. Two–thirds of the world's population is located in the 10/40 Window. In areas of the 10/40 Window, there is only one missionary for every one million people. In the year 2000 there were over one billion Muslims and one billion Hindus in the 10/40 Window. Some of the problems of the 10/40 Window are starvation, disease, economic disaster, religious persecution, government and political breakdown, and insufficient living conditions. Far above all of these, is the need of the gospel of Christ. The gospel is the hope for all nations, including the ones in the 10/40 Window.[1]

- More than 95% of the world's unreached peoples live in this area.
- The 10/40 Window outlines the heartlands of the major non–Christian religions of the world— Islam, Hinduism, Buddhism, Shintoism, and Confucianism.
- About 80% of the poorest of the world's poor live in this region, enduring humanity's lowest standards of living.

lay of the land

"A tiny group of believers who have the gospel keep mumbling it over and over to themselves. Meanwhile, millions who have never heard it once fall into the flames of eternal hell without ever hearing the salvation story."– K.P. Yohannan

Consider the following disproportion of the missionaries working in the world and where they are located. The missionary is someone from another culture working in that country. For example, America has one foreign missionary, who has come from another country such as South Korea, working full–time in ministry here for every 2,700 people in the United States.

- *Iran has 1 missionary for every 3 million people*
- *China has 1 missionary for every 700,000 people*
- *India has 1 missionary for every 2 million people*
- *Pakistan has 1 missionary for every 213,000 people*
- *Vietnam has 1 missionary for every 2 million people*
- *Turkey has 1 missionary for every 270,000 people*
- *Bangladesh has 1 missionary for every 250,000 people*

- *America has 1 missionary for every 2,700 People*
- *Mexico has 1 missionary for every 2,300 people*
- *Peru has 1 missionary for every 240 people*
- *Brazil has 1 missionary for every 276 people*
- *Argentina has 1 missionary for every 180 people*[2]

Do you see the distribution problem? America has over 400,000 churches and over 1 million Christian workers. That is one full–time Christian minister (those from both America or from overseas) for every 250 people here. Keith

Green used to say, "America is 5% of the world's population and should only need 5% of the Christians to stay and reach it." Now seriously, how many Christians do you know who looked at the demographics of world evangelization before they decided to buy a house and settle down in the town they grew up in—based on how strategic it was for world evangelization. Not many? What if Coca Cola ran their business the same way the church has distributed its laborers. New facts always demand a new direction. Some facts will change you … forever. The Moravian missionary Count Zinzendorf basically echoed the same idea hundred of years before, saying, *"I have but one passion—it is He, it is He alone. The world is the field and the field is the world; and henceforth that country shall be my home where I can be most used in winning souls for Christ."* What usually happens in the race that believers set out to run? We say, "Ready, set … pass."

"passing" go

I love to look at this picture of the world and the location of the laborers and then ask people, "Is this the way that God wants it?" Is this His doing? Because in the back of the minds of most believers is the idea that we are excused from the responsibility to act until God has "called" us to go somewhere specifically. If that is the case, it passes the blame on to God for the 10/40 Window, as if He is at fault for the millions of unreached. God is sovereign and in control of all things, somehow even the disobedience of His church and their failure to reach the world plays into His greater picture of gaining glory for Himself. But God is not senile. The 10/40 Window is not the result of God accidentally "calling" too many people to Brazil and forgetting about the lost millions headed for Hell in India. It is the result of believers who are meant to live for the journey that pass on "go," assuming that world missions is for an elite group of super saints. The default is then a life lived for themselves and their agendas—a life of exemption which, for some reason, doesn't require a special calling. Todd Ahrend says, "What you refer to as a 'calling,' is what I call a worse blasphemy than taking the Lord's name in vain." Is your only excuse for not currently joining God in His mission in the world and living in safety and comfort found in the idea that He has not verbally told you to do otherwise? One word: lame. Robert Speer said, "There is something wonderfully misleading, full of hallucination and delusion in this business of missionary calls. With many of us it is not a missionary call at all that we are looking for; it is a shove. There are a great many of us who would never hear a call if it came." The gospel has the authority to interrupt our lives including where we choose to live and what we choose to do with our resources. The gospel frees us to do whatever needs to be done in the journey and the facts about the world light the way.

navigate

> "If every Christian is already considered a missionary, then all can stay put where they are, and nobody needs to get up and go anywhere to preach the gospel. But if our only concern is to witness where we are, how will people in unevangelized areas ever hear the gospel? The present uneven distribution of Christians and opportunities to hear the gospel of Christ will continue on unchanged."– C. Gordon Olson

Another problem is navigating the church to the un-reached. People are going, but going to the same places others have already planted a church. They are working in "reached people groups." A few months ago a group of national missions directors for a smaller evangelical denomination in America asked Todd (Ahrend) and I to come and train them in mission mobilization. We took a stroll through their offices before we left for the meeting place. Todd and I noticed a picture on the wall of about fifty old guys. It was a gathering of all the missionaries in their denomination. Behind them was a map of the world and where each of them had served. The last day Todd brought up the picture when speaking to the group of directors. I tried not to let anyone see me tense up. I knew what he was going to say. He asked them, "Why is it that your missionaries have purposefully stayed out of the 10/40 Window?" There was an uncomfortable silence. "It's like you drew the lines and said, 'Whatever you do, don't go here.'" Then there followed an even more awkward few minutes as they tried to explain their missions strategy.

John Maxwell says that leaders "find a way to win." The key idea is that they "find a way." No one just hands out trophies to losers. OK, bad example. But the real victories in life are not laid out for you to just stroll through; they are labored for and worked for. We must see the need, understand the task, and navigate to win. We may be required to brainstorm new ideas, reorganize our resources and take the initiative ourselves to do something no one has ever done. Leaders will find a way to win. The harvest is still plentiful, but those who will labor and do whatever it takes to reach the destination are few. Know the North Star, know the uncharted nations, and live your life by the compass in order to finish the task.

---

1. P. Black, *Lesson 4– What is the 10/40 Window*, http://www.thetravelingteam.org/2000/world/4.shtml .

2. Source Todd M. Johnson, compiled in *The 10 Modules*, 2002, p53.

CHAPTER ELEVEN

Stopping Short

God's mission is about peoples, not just people.

rewriting the end

A college student named Cameron Townsend was a junior when he took a one year trip to Guatemala to deliver Spanish Bibles to people. While he was selling Bibles one day he noticed a guy who took one, and with a confused look, flipped through the pages. Finally the man approached Cameron and instead of asking what he must do to be saved, or where the nearest baptistery was, this is what he said: "If your God is so great, why doesn't he speak my language?" Cameron was stunned to find that this man, though he lived in Guatemala, did not speak Spanish. He and thousands of others spoke other dialects in which the Bible had never been translated. Cameron was so troubled by the fact that there were thousands of these ethnic groups without the scripture in their language that He decided to initiate and find a way to win. He started by calling his mother and telling her he wouldn't be coming home. Cameron allowed the gospel to interrupt the course of his life. He began an organization known today as Wycliffe Bible Translators[1], which has the goal of translating the Bible into every language on the earth. Currently, there are over 3,000 languages without scripture, but 4,000 have at least portions in their dialect, all because Cameron stumbled on the idea of People Groups.

Imagine if someone hired you to survey and map the entire path through a forest, every foot of it. This might not be too difficult. Then, to your surprise, halfway into the forest the road splits ten different ways. Before taking one, you could stand at the edge and try to guess what is down the other nine. You could do an exceptionally thorough job in detailing the map for one of the ten. Or you could go back and rally other surveyors to the task. The point is that all of the roads must be traveled to the end. No stopping short. This is what people like Cameron found out about world missions. We had only sent people to the different continents first, then the political nation states, but even within those there were thousand of hidden peoples, people groups that had their own language, culture, religions and regions that left them cut–off from the gospel. That is what is meant by the term "unreached peoples." The harvest is plentiful but those that will travel the journey to the end are most needed and most rare.

stopping points

A friend of mine uses an analogy to explain how people groups affect world evangelization.[2] Most people think the world is like a pancake. When you pour syrup on a pancake, it's flat, so eventually the syrup begins to spread out and cover the entire pancake right? Most believe that if we just share the gospel enough where we are, it will eventually spread over the whole world. But it won't. The world is more like a waffle, with "pockets" of people known as people groups. The task of world missions is to bless every single pocket with the gospel. In the New Testament, the Greek word for "nations" is the word "ethne." We get our word ethnicity from it. It means something like an ethnic group. The idea is that it is much more specific than the political nation–states we think of such as Indonesia, Turkey, or Nigeria. The broader pancake–looking country has ethne–pockets in it like a waffle. An anthropologist would call this "ethne" a "people group." A people group is the largest group within which the gospel can spread without encountering barriers of understanding or acceptance due to culture, language, geography, etc.[3]

Take the country of India for example. In India there are hundreds of different ethnic pockets of people, but even among those ethnic groups there are divisions made according to the thousands of languages they speak. It gets more complicated. Among one language and ethnic group there are religious divisions that keep people from interacting with one another, and will, at times, even result in violence between neighboring groups. Even among those same ethnic, language, and religion groups there are more divisions: social divisions. In India it is called the Caste System. Basically, what this all results in is over 2,348 people groups in India that see themselves as a unique people from those around them. And because of their differences, most are isolated from the gospel. Even though it may be nearby, the message of Christ may be in a language they don't understand or in a culture that is unaccepted. In other words they have no interaction with those people groups around them who may have the gospel. Someone must cross these cultural boundaries to get it there. This is the work of missions: to take the gospel into each people group. When the Bible speaks of nations, tribes, tongues, or peoples, it is referring to the same mission—the reaching of all people groups.

The promise of God is that "*all nations (people groups) will be blessed through you*" (Genesis 12:1–3). This means that God is infinitely concerned with the reaching of each and every people group that exists. They will one day make up the multicultural worship service seen in Revelation 7:9. Missions is God's great scavenger hunt for all the nations and ethnic groups on the planet that He has created for His glory. What makes someone a missionary is not that they are in a different location, but that they are within a different people group than their own.

So, if God has promised to reach them all and we are commanded to go to them all, we must be familiar with the task remaining and rally the church to the targeting of them all. There are currently 11,227 people groups in the world and about 6,600 of them are considered unreached.[4] Since we are on mission to reach peoples, not just people, the Great Commission is finishable. It is measurable and able to be completed. The question now is: what is an unreached people group?

Ed Dayton says, "It is a people group among which there is no indigenous community of believing Christians with adequate numbers and resources to evangelize their own people. In other words, unreached people groups lack a church that has the numbers and strength to reach their own people. Obviously, if there are no Christians within this group, there will be none who can share the gospel with them. And this is the situation in which we find over 2.4 billion people of the world. They are the people groups in which there is no church that is able to tell them the good news of Jesus Christ."

God is not only concerned with reaching more and more people, but with reaching as many as possible from every people group. I'll borrow an illustration from another author in which he compares the situation to two sinking ocean liners.[5] Pretend for a moment that the promise of the Naval Admiral was that no matter which ship in his fleet went down or was sinking—there would be some rescued from that ship. If he enlisted his crew for that one purpose, what would they do if there were *two* ocean liners sinking at the same time? Do you see the dilemma? After reaching the first sinking ship you might see that there is great need and you could justify staying to save as many as you could from the first ship, rather than going to the second. You could even argue that in the effort and time it required to get to the second ship, you could be a better steward by staying at the first. Perhaps the people at the other ship are unwilling, and this first ship seems to be a fruitful ground for finding desperate swimmers. "There is plenty of need here." However, this was not the Admiral's command. He specifically ordered his crew to save some men from *both ships*, not just one. This is why it is necessary for men to take the rescue boat to each ship. There must be representatives and survivors at the Admiral's celebration from every ship. God has promised to reach some from every tribe, tongue and nation and people. He has enlisted us to rescue them and one day there will be a celebration banquet where all nations and people groups are represented before the throne.

---

1. Cameron Townsend, for full story visit http://www.wycliffe.org/wbt–usa/WBT–hist.htm .
2. Ian Downs, The Worldwide Waffle, *Mission Frontiers*, Jan/Feb 1998 issue.
3. Bruce Koch, Ralph Winter, *The Perspective on the World Christian Movement (Reader)*, 3rd Ed, Paternoster Publishing, 1999, p514.
4. International Missions Board, Global Research Department, *Status of Global Evangelism*, August 2003, p2. Information available for download at http://peoplegroups.org.
5. John Piper, *Let the Nations Be Glad,* Baker Books, 1993, p168.

CHAPTER TWELVE

Perils on the Journey

"The more obstacles you have, the more opportunities there are for God to do something."

— *Clarence W. Jones*

leaving base camp

Remember hurdles? When I was in middle school I ran track for one year, but I was so short that hurdles were out of the question. I took one look at those metal bars and the 2X4 that seemed to come up to my forehead and knew that I had a greater chance of breaking into Fort Knox than launching my skinny little eighth grade stick legs over one of those things. I decided that God must not have "called" me to run the hurdles race. Maybe I could rake the sand in the long–jump pit or something. I told the coach, "Sir, I cannot jump hurdles." The truth is … I never even tried. What is worse is that I probably wouldn't be able to jump a hurdle today, even though I am taller, stronger and healthier, because deep down I've convinced myself that I'm not a hurdle jumper.

Life is full of hurdles. Theodore Roosevelt seemed to have this view of life when he expressed the now famous quote, *"Far better it is to dare mighty things to win glorious triumphs, even though checkered by failure, than to take rank with those poor spirits who neither enjoy much nor suffer much, because they live in the gray twilight that knows not victory nor defeat.*" When it comes to joining God in His work on the earth, most of us face a couple of common issues, or hurdles, which either make us hesitate, fail, or never try at all. You need to learn these perils so you can navigate your way through to the destination. A normal list would include family disapproval, fear of support raising, dating issues, worldly agendas, lack of accountability, financial debt, selfishness, or just ignorance to God's heart for the world, and uncertainty to God's will for our lives. If we are going to join God in the journey, we must anticipate the hurdles and perils ahead of us. The first hurdles you have to jump are the ones in your mind. God created you as you are for the journey and He intends on using you just as you are for His purposes. You can't finish the journey if you never leave the base camp. Don't allow yourself to settle for life in the outer court.

vines

There are good vines and bad vines. Sometimes a vine can be a lifesaving source of stability that you can swing from like Tarzan, avoiding the dangers below. A vine can be strong enough to pull you out of a pit or quick sand. However, other vines have a will of their own. They don't help you on the journey. They work against you. If they get the chance, they can cling around your feet and legs until you are completely immobilized. The sad thing about the journey is that family, even though designed to be a source of strong support, can sometimes be one of the greatest obstacles.

Jesus warned us that our own family could become a peril to those seeking to follow Him. "*Do not think that I came to bring peace on the earth; I did not come to bring peace, but a sword. For I came to set a man against his father, and a daughter against her mother, and a daughter–in–law against her mother–in–law; and a man's enemies will be the members of his household. He who loves father or mother more than Me is not worthy of Me; and he who loves son or daughter more than Me is not worthy of Me. And he who does not take his cross and follow after Me is not worthy of Me. He who has found his life will lose it, and he who has lost his life for My sake will find it" (Matthew 10:34–39).*

If you are going to begin the journey, you will have to make the decision to travel even if you travel alone. Just like the hymn, *I Have Decided to Follow Jesus,* says, "Though none go with me, I still will follow. No turning back, no turning back." I can't believe how many times I've met students like David. David came up to me after my message on missions and said, "Two weeks ago, I surrendered my life completely to the Lord and to full–time ministry."

"Great, that's awesome!" I replied.

To which he goes on to tell me, "Yeah, that's what my mom said too, except she added, 'Anything but missions!'"

One of the greatest obstacles right now to the Great Commission is Christian parents. I can't tell you how many horror stories I've heard from young adults about the manipulating, threatening and bargaining their parents will do to try to keep them safe and at home. I just begin to picture the vines growing up around the beautiful feet of these potential world changers. Parents claim that God is sovereign and that He is working all things for the good, but then deny it by attempting to be in control of the safety and even the direction of their children's lives. Parents, like the clinging vines, can have a "will of their own." There is nothing more damaging in a young person's life than to be forced to choose between honoring their parents and obeying the Lord. I do not believe that family *always* comes first. That is an American idea, not a Christian one. *"And everyone who has left houses or brothers or sisters or father or mother or children or farms for My name's sake, will receive many times as much, and will inherit eternal life"* (*Matthew 19:29*). When Jesus spoke about the persecution and trials we would face, He always included relationships. Parents with a vision for the world and a heart for the Great Commission can be a great strength, but those that haven't been captured by the North Star will not understand. They may even work against your journey.

Now don't start picturing yourself hacking away at the vine with a machete, that's not the answer either. It is not completely your parent's fault. They, like many of us, just got a bad pass from the generation before. They weren't told their purpose for which God created them. They weren't taught that they were part of a missionary family. David reminds the families of the church about the commands of God to teach the next generation. *"He commanded our fathers that they should teach them to their children, that the generation to come might know, even the children yet to be born, that they may arise and tell them to their children"* (*Psalms 78:6*). Our duty is not to blame resistant parents, which can sometimes be a smokescreen for disobedience. We are to take the responsibility, run with it well, and pass it well to the next generation. If you begin the journey and find that the vines are against you—you are not an exception. Family discouragement is normal, but is not always permanent. Pray that they would become a mighty vine, holding fast for you in times of sinking and danger. Ultimately, the best way for you to model Christ–likeness to your parents is to show them that they, being "branches" like you, must yield to the true vine. *"I am the vine … apart from Me you can do nothing"* (*John 15:5*).

f o g

"For you will no longer remember the oracle of the Lord, because every man's own word will become the oracle, and you have perverted the words of the living God, the Lord of hosts, our God."– Jeremiah 23:36

One day in college, I was sharing the gospel with guys in a specific dorm on my campus when I met Shane. He was an average small–town guy from Oklahoma. As we began to talk about what he believed about God, I was prepared for the usual ideas of what was true or not. Maybe he would dispute the Bible, or perhaps he thought he was a Christian already. But Shane was different. He felt the freedom to create his own truth. Basically he was somewhere between Hinduism and Christianity, believing that you were saved by faith in Jesus alone, apart from works, but that if you didn't receive Christ in this life—you would be reincarnated over and over until you got it right. Nice idea. I give him credit for his loving heart and his creativity. Shane was my first taste of the fog that was going to settle over the hearts and minds of this generation—relative truth.

Tolerance and relativism are now the new icons of the west. It is drilled in by the media, the schools, and even some so–called churches. The danger disguised in the language of religious tolerance is the greatest emerging threat to evangelicals and the work of the Great Commission. I recently heard the director of the CIA speak at a graduation and make the claim that religious intolerance is the cause of most of the suffering going on in the world. A few sentences later he encouraged us to make prayer a priority—what? Do you see how confusing and foggy this is to the world that just soaks it in? As I am writing this, *Time* magazine has just released its latest issue with a cross on the cover and the title, *"Should Christians Convert Muslims?"* The article goes on to name agencies and mobilization groups, with the intent on exposing these "radical" evangelical groups. I frequently find myself warning Christians that there will soon be a day when evangelism will be labeled a hate crime in our cities.

The college students that I meet are lost in this gray fog of trying to figure out whether all the religions are really just relative truths for others born in other cultures. There is a surprising number of what I call "closet universalists" in the church. *Universalists* are people who believe that there is universal salvation for everyone, and in the end everyone is saved; nobody goes to Hell. This sounds great. It flows from a kind heart that desires, as God does, for none to perish. However, scripture is clear that there is one way and one name under Heaven by which men must be saved, (John 14:6, Acts 4:12) and that "he who does not believe has been judged already, because he has not believed in the name of the only begotten Son of God." (John 3:18) Therefore, those that have never heard the name of Jesus, the unreached peoples of the 10/40 Window and the world, stand condemned already, and in need of the gospel. The "closet universalist" holds their opposing belief, not because they have thought through it, but because they haven't. It is sort of a default teaching, more gossiped than taught, but spreading in the church anyway. When confronted with the truth and exclusive claims of Jesus, most come out of the "closet" to their own surprise that they were in that camp. We must help clear the fog with the truth, not because we are intolerant of others, but because of our love for them and our desire that they be saved in the way Jesus provided—the only way.

making shelter

"It is said that there are no atheists in foxholes. If that is true, we must also ask the question, 'Are there really any true believers in bomb–shelters?'"– Erwin McManus

Some have left the journey, because they have stopped to build shelters. We have a tendency to gravitate toward safety and comfort and away from risk and danger. There is nothing that will hinder us more from walking the journey and joining God in His global mission than our own fear of taking risk for the kingdom of God. There's no such thing as a portable bomb shelter in this journey. Safety and the journey are opposing directions. *"Let us go with him outside the camp" (Hebrews 13:13).* To follow Christ where He is headed is to move toward danger and take risks. We must leave the camp. There is never a guarantee that the journey will be safe, or that all will turn out well, at least in the short run. Like Esther we must say,*"If I perish, I perish" (Esther 4:16).* Unfortunately we get our values from the world when it comes to looking out for number one. We are almost taught to avoid and fear risk, even by the church. Deep down, at the heart of all pursuits, degrees, careers, and possessions, we are all still trying to save our lives, not lose them. God finds the plans we make out of our desire for safety so contrary to the life He has created us for that He calls it rebellion.

"Woe to the rebellious children," declares the Lord, "Who execute a plan, but not Mine, and make an alliance, but not of My Spirit, in order to add sin to sin; who proceed down to Egypt without consulting Me, to take refuge in the safety of Pharaoh and to seek shelter in the shadow of Egypt! Therefore the safety of Pharaoh will be your shame and the shelter in the shadow of Egypt, your humiliation" (Isaiah 30:1–3).

I remember when I was starting to get a heart for the world. I had read some books and could tell you what the 10/40 Window was. I was hanging out with this radical missions guy named Kevin. Kevin had been shot at in Sudan by helicopters, Muslims had killed several pastors before his very eyes, and since then he had been back to Sudan, smuggling in Bibles and supplies to the persecuted church. We were at my pastor's house talking about what was going on in the world. Everything was going great until Kevin, who was really excited about his next trip into Sudan, said, "Claude, why don't you come with me?" I think that I audibly gulped. Some color must have left my face. Either that or the frozen stare I drilled back at Kevin gave away my heart. Before I could even come up with a response, Kevin had already seen me exposed. I left that night, not so much disappointed that I was a total coward, but disappointed that I wasn't who I wanted to be. I knew the right stuff to say, but I didn't really own the words. Be careful, the heart is deceitful. Agreement does not equal obedience. Knowledge is not an adequate substitute for real involvement with our lives. There are very few times that the gospel interrupted someone's life in the Bible that it didn't result in moving them toward risk and danger. You may have noticed this, but have you digested it? How will you reconcile your life to the promise that, *"Indeed, all who desire to live godly in Christ Jesus will be persecuted"* (2 Timothy 3:12). It is easy for your heart to trick you into trying to save your life, but if you let it, it will certainly cost you the life you were meant to experience: the life on the journey. There have been times, both overseas and here that I have made choices that have moved me toward risk. Twice there were situations that actually became very dangerous. Both times I walked away feeling an incredible sense of freedom. I was free because I had refused to let fear keep me paralyzed. Even if I would have died, at least I was fully alive.

rabbit trails

"The reason there is a 10/40 Window is Christians are busy doing great Christian things."

There is a theme laid out for us to make our paths straight. It calls us to watch where we are going. There is a danger if we don't—rabbit trails. We are to walk purposefully. This journey has to be conquered, and only the aggressive attention to the North Star will keep us on the true path. The shortest distance between two points is a straight line. The fastest way for us to fulfill the Great Commission is to live life by the compass and follow the path "straight" to the destination. Listen to the word of the Lord.

"I will lead them; I will make them walk by streams of waters, on a <u>straight path</u> in which they will not stumble; for I am a father to Israel" (Jeremiah 31:9)

"In all your ways acknowledge Him, and He will make your <u>paths straight</u>" (Proverbs 3:6).

"Let your eyes look directly ahead, let your gaze be fixed <u>straight in front of you</u>" (Proverbs 4:25).

"Folly is joy to him who lacks sense, but a man of understanding <u>walks straight</u>" (Proverbs 15:21).

"When the angels had gone away from them into Heaven, the shepherds began saying to one another, '<u>Let us go straight to Bethlehem</u> then, and see this thing that has happened which the Lord has made known to us'"(Luke 2:15).

"Make <u>straight paths</u> for your feet, so that the limb which is lame may not be put out of joint, but rather be healed" (Hebrews 12:13).

If only Rebecca and I would have walked straight through the Forbidden City, we would have made it inside in time. We wouldn't have missed out on the real Forbidden City. We got distracted during the journey. We took a rabbit trail and had to settle for only seeing the outer courts. Some will not join God on the journey because they have already gone too far down a rabbit trail. They have given themselves for so long to other agendas and other values that they are past the point of no return. The roots have grown so deeply that they cannot bring themselves to uproot. If you walk down the wrong path on the journey and fail to allow the gospel to interrupt your life soon enough, you are in danger of getting lost. The weeds begin to grow up behind you, covering the path that leads back to the journey God designed you for. The heart has an amazing ability to cloud the mind. Like the weeds, the heart slowly removes the memory of the journey from our minds. As a dream when you awake, within a few moments what seemed so real is unattainable. A few moments in the outer courts and before you know it you are stuck. When I say "past the point of no return," it is not because God doesn't allow us to return, but because it is the paralysis in our own mind that holds us. You are simply too far removed to allow the gospel to interrupt the course of your life. You could compare it to the rich young ruler who was asked to sell everything and follow Jesus. It wasn't that his possessions where sinful, but that they had gripped him. It isn't hopeless, but in order to make it back to the path it will take some backtracking and sacrifice. God warns us to take the "straight path" and not get sidetracked by illusion of the glitter offered by the world's paths.

Most rabbit trails are not worldly things, but Christian ones. There are many great distractions in the outer courts. It looks so much like the real thing. The irony is that we were so busy buying souvenirs of the Forbidden City that we didn't even make it into the real thing. We can fool our friends with our pictures of the outer courts, but a life lived in the outer court can't fool God. Christians are busy doing countless good things; however their pursuits are, unfortunately, not aligned with God's purpose of gathering people from every nation.

Do you believe that there is a way of doing life, even "ministry," that could actually be working against the Great Commission? Jesus said, *"He who is not with Me is against Me; and he who does not gather with Me scatters" (Matthew 12:30)*. What does it mean to not be "with Him?" Does it mean be moral? Plenty of atheists are more moral than most. Does it mean to believe? The demons believe and shudder, but are not working "with Him" to "gather." What it means to be *with Him* is to follow Jesus in where He is headed and to work for His purposes on the earth, *gathering* the nations back to Himself. Jesus is calling us to join in the one thing God is doing, laboring toward the one North Star of His global purpose. If you are not working toward this, the gathering of all the nations, it doesn't matter what "Christian" thing you are doing—it is actually *scattering*. The two are mutually exclusive. It may be working against His mission by consuming time, resources, and people with the rabbit trail of good Christian activities. The enemy of the best is often the good. The enemy of the gospel is the Christian that does everything but share it. The reason the 10/40 Window still exists is Christians are busy doing great Christian things. *"Therefore, since we have so great a cloud of witnesses surrounding us, let us also lay aside every encumbrance and the sin which so easily entangles us, and let us run with endurance the race that is set before us" (Hebrews 12:1)*. We are commanded to throw off, not just sin, but everything that entangles us from running the race. God may desire for you to throw off even the great Christian plans that are not aligned with contributing to His gathering of the peoples; first because they work against Jesus, and secondly because you were designed for His journey not yours. To take your own path, even a "Christian" looking one, is to reject God's purpose for your life. *"But the Pharisees and the lawyers rejected God's purpose for themselves, not having been baptized by John"* (Luke 7:30). Don't reject God's purpose for your life. When you fight against the magnetic force of true north on your life, you fight against God's purpose for your life. With all you do, align yourself with the true north, the gathering of the nations. Otherwise, you may be part of the scattering.

the dead end dream

"But those who want to get rich fall into temptation and a snare and many foolish and harmful desires which plunge men into ruin and destruction" (1 Timothy 6:9).

Addictions to things such as money and status and comfort begin to deceive the mind like other addictions, so that you rarely perceive the severity of the problem. The heart is deceitful and it will betray you if you sell out for treasure here. That is why it is important to guard your heart. Jesus tells us that where your treasure is, there your heart will be. In other words, the best way we can guard our hearts is to control what we truly treasure. This addiction to the American Dream can begin to control our lives like a drug. The American Dream is deadly to the potential World Christian. The Bible describes it as a "snare" on the journey, plunging men into "ruin and destruction." There is a subtleness to the American Dream that has snuck up on the church. Now you can go to church, live a moral life, raise a good family, but ultimately live for yourself—the picket fence, the two cars, the perfect house, 2.5 kids and the extended family less than a mile away, working for status and more toys, more respect in the workplace, more praise of men. That is the pursuit of most "normal" Christian families you and I know. Something deadly to the work of evangelism and the work that God wants to do in our lives is the substitution of Heaven's rewards for the lesser, sweet–n–low version of rewards that we settle for here on earth. It is deadly to evangelism because no one wants to follow a church full of people claiming to live for Heaven, but running after the same carrots they chase after. It is hypocritical and duplicitous. Also, it is deadly to our sanctification because it is a trap. It lures us away from the path of God to the dead ends of the world. All sin is the replacing of God's design for meeting our needs with Satan's lesser satisfying methods of meeting our needs. Once we begin to taste the temptation of the American Dream, its hold grows on us so greatly that we cannot recognize the better pleasures that God offers for us in Jesus. The drug of the American Dream kills the brain cells of eternal thinking. The longer you tarry there, the more your mind shrinks from living for greater things. The North Star of the American Dream is emptiness, and its compass is the love of money and the praise of men.

> "Beware that you do not forget the Lord your God by not keeping His commandments and His ordinances and His statutes which I am commanding you today; otherwise, when you have eaten and are satisfied, and have built good houses and lived in them, and when your herds and your flocks multiply, and your silver and gold multiply, and all that you have multiplies, then your heart will become proud and you will forget the Lord your God who brought you out from the land of Egypt, out of the house of slavery" (Deuteronomy 8:11–17).

CHAPTER THIRTEEN

Running with Your Head Down

Humility involves a Copernican revolution of the soul, the realization that the universe does not revolve around us.

– John Ortberg

running to catch up

"All that is necessary for evil to triumph is for good men to do nothing."– Unknown

There is an urgency to our journey—it's not a stroll. There must be a swift intentionality to our steps. We must take the initiative to reach the world in this generation—for several reasons. The population of the world as I write this is 6.3 billion people according to the U.S. Census website population clock. I frequently check the "pop clock" when I'm online, because the number excites me and haunts me at the same time. The population of the world is exploding, growing at over 6 million people per month. Despite what you may see around you, there is an incredible amount of people on the planet right now. This scares me because if we hesitate with the gospel, millions of lives are at stake.

You may have heard this statistic, but there are more people alive today than have ever lived and died in all of history combined. This means that if you added up all the people who have ever lived from Adam until the late 1900's, they would still be less than the 6.3 billion on the planet right now. The growth curve has taken a sharp turn upward. This means that our generation will be responsible for where the majority of people are going to spend eternity. Does that make sense? There are more people alive today; therefore, there will be more people in either Heaven or Hell from this generation than there are from any other time in history. What a weight of responsibility our generation has—and on the other hand, what an opportunity! This is also what excites me about the pop clock. Could it be that God has allowed the disobedience of the church to work into His plan in this way? Meaning that God not only has the opportunity to reach all peoples of the earth, but He has the opportunity to redeem more people than ever before in history. His triumph will not be a pathetic few from every nation, but a vast army of worshippers, a "great multitude" made up of every people group—if we seize our moment in the journey. The time to begin the journey is today. Mildred Cable said, *"God provides the men and women needed for each generation."* In order to rise to the occasion of our generation, we must lift up our eyes off of ourselves. No more running with our heads down focused on ourselves. We must lift up our eyes, as Jesus said, to see the harvest. It is not many more months until the harvest is ready. The fields are ripe for the harvest right now. (John 4:35)

running up the bill

> *"All the blessings of God's resources without the urgency to live for His purpose on the journey become a terrible waste."*

The population is not the only thing on the rise. The affluence and prosperity of the West has made us the most blessed and most paralyzed church in history. I wish at times that I didn't know about the amount of money that churches spend on gymnasiums, electronic marquees, fountains, new carpet and a Lexus for the pastor. It's no wonder that more and more people are "surrendering" to the ministry. There was actually a pastor in California who the IRS investigated because of the size and value of his home. Basically the church offering goes countless places besides to the unreached. Bob Sjogren, in his book Unveiled At Last,[1] gives the rough figure of how every dollar given in the offering plate in the evangelical churches of the U.S. is spent. Ninety–six cents goes right back into the American church. The other four cents are divided up among reached areas and unreached. Do you think it was fifty–fifty? The reality is that 3.5 cents goes to the reached people groups. Have you ever seen those pennies that have the cross cut out of the middle? The scraps from those go to reaching the unreached peoples of the world—just kidding. But the fact is less than half a cent of every dollar given goes to people groups in the 10/40 Window. Christians spend more on dog food than they give to missions every year. Do you want to hear one more that will make you cry? Church janitors embezzle more money (picking up quarters and change out of the pews) than is given to world missions. Jesus gave us the formula for developing a heart like His for the world. *"Where your treasure is there your heart will be also" (Matthew 6:21)*. The compass directs the way we use our resources. If we run with our head down and spend money only on local needs, we are in danger of working against Him and His work on the earth. God has blessed us to be a channel of blessing to the nations. *"God blesses us, that all the ends of the earth may fear Him" (Psalms 67:7)*.

running all the bases

"Christianity without discipleship is always Christianity without Christ."–Dietrich Bonhoeffer

I've noticed something else over the past few years as I have labored on a college campus and traveled the U.S. speaking to college students. Everyone has his or her bandwagon. They have one conviction about some issue that they always find a way to bring up, and they are always attempting to persuade others to their way of thinking. This is especially true in Christian culture, because it makes people feel spiritual. Most of the time they are right and their convictions are good. In this student generation, I've seen missions become one of those bandwagons. Of course I'm not opposed to beating the missions drum. The problem is that missions has become the 'quick fix' spirituality that some newly converted, zealous, but unbroken believers have found to be their ticket to the head of the pack. He reads a book, hears one talk, memorizes some statistics and jargon, and next thing you know he is criticizing the pastor and every other ministry because they don't share his world vision. Unfortunately, this disgruntled Christian is mistaken for a leader and given authority to reward his puffed up attitude.

What went wrong? Was this the way Jesus designed it? No. What's missing is discipleship, the process of being mentored and taught the basics of following Jesus by another human being. It is humbling to be taught. One of the first qualities I look for in a believer is teachability. If someone is unteachable, self–reliant, and so independent that they have nothing to learn from anyone, I don't care how much they know or what they have done, they are useless. On the other hand, a lifelong learner is of far greater potential, even if he knows very little at the time. Unfortunately, most of the students I meet have no one discipling them personally. They may be in a Bible study or cell group that they float into once a week for an hour, but this is not discipleship. We have replaced obedience with knowledge. Just because you know the North Star doesn't mean you are on the journey.

There are four phases that we cycle through in the journey guided by the North Star. If we look at the life of Jesus we see that He moved His disciples through these four phases. The first is evangelism, bringing them to believe in Him as the Messiah. The next phase is establishing, grounding them in the basics of the Christian life. After awhile, some followers proved themselves to be faithful men and were selected for special training, or equipping. Only after this filtering process did He extend them to the nations on their own. Dr. Bill Jones, Bible professor at Columbia International University, uses the analogy of first, second, third base, and home plate. A team can have more runners on base and lose the game. Discipleship without extending them to the nations is just as fruitless. To win you must score. The only way to score is to round all the bases. That was the Lord's method; *evangelize, establish, equip, extend.* We also see that the early Church modeled this. Just read through Acts and see the pattern of developing believers, training them, and then sending them to the nations.

Early on in the development of the Church you see the phases. First was evangelizing when Peter said, *"Repent and be baptized...and the Lord added to their number daily those who were being saved"* (Acts 2:38, 47). Next was establishing.*"Those who accepted his message were baptized ... they devoted themselves to the apostles' teaching and to the fellowship, to the breaking of bread and to prayer"* (Acts 2:41, 42). They were established in the basics of the Christian life: fellowship, communion, prayer and the apostles' teaching from Scripture. When the time was right, they began to equip leaders."*Choose seven men from among you who are known to be full of the Spirit and wisdom. We will turn this responsibility over to them*" (Acts 6:3, 7). These weren't just waiters, they were people set apart and trained for the ministry. Finally, they had to decide whether the gospel should be extended outside the Jews. *"I now realize how true it is that God does not show favoritism, but accepts men from every nation who fear him and do what is right"* (Acts 10:34–48).

After this, we soon see them reaching out to the Gentiles and starting back at evangelizing; phase one. "*Some of them went to Antioch and began to speak to Greeks also, telling them the good news about the Lord Jesus ... a great number of people believed and turned to the Lord*" (Acts 11:20–21). Next was phase two, establishing. "*So for a whole year Barnabas and Saul met with the Church and taught great numbers of people*" (Acts 11:22–26). Now they selected and equipped leaders to take ministry roles in the church. "*In the Church of Antioch there were prophets and teachers (trained men)*" (Acts 13:1). Finally, they decided the gospel shouldn't just stay in Antioch but was to be sent out and extended by missionaries. "*So after they had fasted and prayed, they placed their hands on them and sent them off*" (Acts 13:3–4).

We even see a quick summary of these phases with Paul among the church in Thessalonica. There was evidence of evangelizing. "*For we know, brothers loved by God, that he has chosen you, because our gospel came to you not simply with words, but also with power ...*" (1 Thessalonians 1:4–5). There was establishing. "*You know how we lived among you for your sake. You became imitators of us and of the Lord*" (1 Thessalonians 1:6). Leaders were equipped. "*And so you became a model to all the believers in Macedonia and Achaia*" (1 Thessalonians 1:7). Finally, people were extended. "*The Lord's message rang out from you not only in Macedonia and*

Achaia– your faith in God has become known everywhere" (1 *Thessalonians* 1:8).

This was the Lord's method, and the early Church's method: *evangelize, establish, equip, and extend.* A friend from a mission agency told me that at their last candidate training, they were getting ready to explain how to share Christ in a Muslim culture, when one student raised his hand and said, "Uh... I've never shared Christ in my own culture." My friend also told me that they send people home all the time because they are not established or equipped for the work. They have zeal, seminary degrees and knowledge, but lack the real life model. Without this grounding, the missionary has nothing to reproduce once he goes overseas. He may be able to lead them to Christ, but as far as knowing how to teach them the basics of the Christian life, (how to share their faith, scripture memory, Bible study, prayer, fellowship, accountability), he has no experience to draw from. He has never seen someone trained in his own life. He is unable to reproduce a growing Christian that can help others to grow. Even if he does plant a church, the people will be dependent on him, because he lacks the ability to establish and equip them to lead. Or worse, he will teach them that intellectual knowledge is the equivalent of spirituality, and reproduce his own independent spirit into those he desires to train.

The goal of discipleship is to multiply. Jesus could have led large crusades to win thousands of people to the Kingdom, but He didn't. Instead He chose to invest His life deeply into a few faithful men. He knew the result would be far more impacting for the future if He could train some disciplemakers. The missionary Paul adopted the same vision. In 2 Timothy 2:2, he exhorts Timothy to entrust the things he learned from Paul to, "faithful men, who are able to teach others also." Four generations of discipleship in one verse: Paul to Timothy, to faithful men, to the others they would train. There is power in multiplication. If you led one person to Christ each day for 33 years, that would be over 12,000 people. But instead, let's say that you led one person to Christ and discipled them in a year so that they could go out and win and train others, and that this process of evangelizing, establishing, equipping, and extending was built into each one. Even if it just started with you, within 33 years you would have reached over 8 billion people. Jesus knew that this was a powerful thing to give His life to.

running your mouth

> "Christians don't tell lies, they just go to church and sing them."– A.W. Tozer

There is another way that we have attempted to run the race with our head down, focused on ourselves. It is the not–so–recent emergence of a new god– "worship." It's just like on the Titanic, when the ship was going down. People are perishing and the small stringed quartet decides to keep playing, not out of joy for the situation, but to forget it. There is a safe kind of disconnection in the singing and worship movement. It has a pretense of obedience but lacks the life to match. It's easier to sing about obeying that to obey. It is easier to sing about asking for the nations, than to actually take a few minutes and ask God for them.

In Germany during the Holocaust, when Hitler was on a mission to wipe out the Jewish people, they would transport captured Jews to their concentration camps on train cars. As the trains would pass through towns, the people packed into the cattle cars would cry out in the hope that people would come to their aid. One church located close to the tracks was disturbed each Sunday morning by the sounds of the people wailing. So finally the church calculated the exact time that the train passed. Then they began to schedule a hymn for the congregation to sing right when the train would go by, in order to drown out the sounds of the people. It was said that at times you could still hear the sound of the people over the organ and singing—so "we would just sing louder."

Our own singing has made us deaf. The way to worship on the journey is not to stand still and admire one aspect of God's glory, but to move forward around the corners to find more and more to praise God for. True worship and admiration will draw you to experience more of the journey. Walk further, in order to worship further.

Beware of this shallow worship substitute, which is really just singing, and not the worship that the Bible describes. Singing is no substitute for a life of sacrifice and devotion to the journey. This experience–seeking generation is hooked on the emotion of worship like a drug—moving from one band to the next, always looking for a bigger, better concert. One of my favorite worship leaders, Ross King, who has a great view of what danger this idol has become, wrote in his song "Clear the Stage" these challenging words to our worship–worshipping culture. These are the opening verses in the song.

> "Clear the stage and set the sound and lights ablaze
> if that's the measure you must take to crush the idols.
>
> Jerk the pews and all the decorations too,
> until the congregation's few then have revival.
>
> Tell your friends that this is where the party ends,
> until you're broken for your sins you can't be social.
>
> Then seek the Lord and wait for what He has in store
> and know that great is your reward so just be hopeful.

'Cause you can sing all you want to, you can sing all you want to,

you can sing all you want to and don't get me wrong, but worship is more than a song.[2]

Todd Ahrend, who has traveled the U.S. and seen hundreds of college worship meetings, also sees the man–centeredness of worship in the Christian sub–culture. He says this on the topic of true worship.

What might be happening is that we bring in good musicians, it draws a crowd, and we say, "Look, people are coming, it must be God, everybody is worshipping!" No, everybody is singing and the majority leaves lacking. Why? Because the students come not to lay down their sin and suffering, but to forget it for a while. Pop in a Vineyard CD and drive down the road. No different than when I was a nonchristian and I couldn't stand quietness, it's just now I Christianize it, turn up my radio, and zone out while I drive. Isn't it amazing how many will go to a worship conference and not a missions conference. Culturally, the first revolves around singing and the second revolves around giving up your life. As I search the scriptures I love what the apostle Paul says about worship in Romans 12:1–2, *"Therefore I urge you brethren, by the mercies of God, to present your bodies a living and holy sacrifice, acceptable to God, which is your spiritual act of worship."* If you cornered Paul, what would he say in regards to worship? I don't necessarily think he would say it is a singing thing. According to him worship is a holy living issue. To turn away from pornography, that is worship. To take every thought captive, that is worship. To lay aside your dreams and talents, that is worship. To forgive each other, that is worship. To walk out of the church more like Jesus, that is worship. Next time we worship God we don't have to go buy a CD with some slow songs on it. Instead we need to tie ourselves on the altar and present our bodies as a living and holy sacrifice.[3]

It is strange that the outer courts are drawing the greatest crowds to sing of the glory of the inner city—although they have never been there. Neil McClendon says it's just like a travel agent. There are many that are just making a business out of trying to sell you a ticket to a place they have never been. If only those in the outer courts could lift up their eyes, pull back and leave the singing to experience the real thing. Worship is something we do when we travel the journey with joy and with determination. When you are living life by the compass each step is an act of worship.

1. Bob Sjogren, *Run with the Vision*, YWAM Publishing, 1992, p139.
2. Ross King, words by Ross King, *Clear the Stage*, from the album *And All the Decorations Too*, 2002, http://www.rosskingmusic.com.
3. Todd Ahrend, *What is Worship*, article from The Traveling Team website, http://www.thetravelingteam.org/2000/articles/wiw.shtml

Your Life

"I am convinced the great tragedy is not the sins that we commit, but the life that we fail to live. For a lot of us the most spiritual thing we can do is to do something—to turn right when we want to turn left. At worst a passive life is only pitied, yet God counts it as a tragedy when we choose to simply watch life rather that live it."

–Erwin McManus

CHAPTER FOURTEEN

Living by the Compass

Living life by the compass is living life on purpose, directing the daily decisions of your life by the true north of God's purposes toward the world.

set your course

In the final scene from the movie The Search for Bobby Fisher, there is a perfect picture of what it looks like to set a course. Bobby Fisher, the greatest chess player in the world, has trained the story's center character, a young boy. The boy is engaged in the championship game of chess, and of course he is playing against his bitter rival. All is thought to be lost when he loses his queen early in the game. Then Bobby, looking intently, studying each of their moves, exclaims to the parents, "He's just won." The victory is sealed. There is only one problem. It is fifteen moves away. The question is: Will the boy focus on the pieces, or will he take in the bigger picture and "see it?"

You may not be a chess player, but here are some tips. The way to lose at chess is to play trying not to lose your pieces. Playing one reaction at a time, trying to save your pieces, will result in losing the entire game. In the end you will lose all the pieces that you were trying so hard to protect. The way to win is to see the big picture and to move with a big picture in mind. You must sacrifice pieces at times to lure your opponent to places in order to win in the end. He who tries to save his pieces will lose them, but he, who uses his pieces for the big picture, even though he loses some, will in the end win the game.

The way to win in life and to finish the journey is to live with a vision of the end. Even though you are a great distance away you "see it." Is there a gravitational pull on your vision to the true north of what God is doing? Do you have a clear picture of what God is doing that you can set the course of your life by? Are you "beginning with the end in mind?" This is what I mean by living life by the compass. It is living life on purpose, directing the daily decisions of your life by the true north of God's purposes toward the world. The victory is sure; it is fifteen moves away—do you "see it?"

Earlier we talked about the difference between seeking a map versus a compass. The compass is more valuable by far. A person lost in the woods doesn't need a map; they need a compass—direction. We can check a map by the compass and see whether or not it is headed in the right direction. Our maps will change from season to season in our lives, but the compass in unchanging. The compass is the same for all men. It always gives the direction to true north no matter what your language, your country, your social status, your family, or your ability. It stands as a firm standard. Seek the compass; check the maps. Living life by the compass means letting God's agenda and the North Star of His heart become the guiding principle for all our decisions. We can choose our steps based on what takes us closer towards the right destination. If you think about it, a person using a compass is allowed to run the journey more efficiently, taking harder climbs that may be a shortcut. He can run more swiftly, trusting confidently in the true direction of the compass. He can run with more perseverance. He is not left to hack away at the jungle, not sure if he is even going the right way. He runs with the energy of hope through trials and the "thick brush" of life, because he labors in faith and with a Christ–magnifying expectation of seeing the destination. Living by the compass gives us direction for our journey and it grows our own faith in the journey along the way. As we obey, it increases the magnetic force of due north on our hearts.

> *"You can do something other than working with God in His purpose, but it will always be something lesser, and you couldn't come up with something better."– Steve Hawthorne*

make a life

> *It is the millions of small decisions not centered around God's global purpose that produces the millions of small Christians not living for God's global purpose.*

No one sets sail for smallness. They drift there. Like a dead fish that floats up to the shore—they don't make choices or swim. They just let life and the waves of social pressure carry them along. The church has been caught up in the mainstream and is too weak to fight the current. It is the passive defaulting to the world in the everydayness of life that produces small people living for small things.

Have you ever wondered what people will say about your life? I have. A few years ago, I was with a few friends passing through Tyler, TX. We decided to stop and see the gravestones of two Christian legends buried there: Keith Green and Leonard Ravenhill. We pull into a small, unkept cemetery, and I was the first out of the car. I had been pondering what could be written on the graves of two men who impacted so many lives during their days on the earth. There they were—Keith and Ravenhill, not even five feet from each other. When I came to Ravenhill's, I found more than I expected. On one side it simply said "Ravenhill" and on the other an inscription. It wasn't a statement about his life, but an inspection of mine. It simply read, *"Are the things you are living for, worth Christ dying for?"* It would have been no less powerful of a moment if there had been a mirror reflecting the image of my soul. A truly meaningful life makes an impact that outlives the person. There is more of a message to the world in this one grave than in the lives of many well–known Christians today. I left there that day not wishing for a greater gravestone, but for a greater life—one worthy of marking.

The secret to making your life count for God's global purpose is not found in trying to master everything, but by being mastered by His North Star and letting it grip your life. There are a few things in life that are worth living for and even dying for. We must daily align our lives with the journey's end. Keep your eyes on the destination, keep walking, and the path will always be beneath you. Living by the compass does not mean that you will necessarily become a foreign missionary. The goal is that we become what David Bryant termed a "World Christian," a follower of Jesus who is aligning their life with God's heart for the world. Being a World Christian is an issue of lordship and lifestyle, and location. You must have all three. Location in the world does not make you involved in God's Great Commission. Living a simple lifestyle does not mean you are living to free up resources for the work of God's church in the world. Without lordship the other two are useless. Our lifestyle and location must be the out–flowing of the lordship of Jesus over our lives. The gospel has the authority, the lordship, to interrupt our lifestyle and our location. Missions isn't about where you are going with your summer. It's about where you are going with your life.

living and lordship

There are two significant, decisive questions that I have asked my wife, Rebecca, that have really shaped our journey in life together. The first was when I asked her to marry me. It was huge for me because she could have shut me down, and it was intimidating for her because she was giving up her last name and her rights and committing to follow me wherever that would lead. The second vital question came a year later. We were married now, and I was preparing to begin a Masters degree. However, there was another road emerging as we learned about God's heart for the world. Finally, right before I was to begin my Masters program we went to hear a missions speaker, the one that talked about the Moravians. This is the rest of that story. It was such a powerful moment that I knew what God was guiding me toward. The decision was made for me in that class that night; I was going to allow God to interrupt the course of my life and I was going to walk the journey. There was only one problem. I needed to let my wife next to me in on our new life direction. So I turned to Rebecca, and it wasn't so much a question that I asked as it was me telling her where I was headed, and her deciding whether she could adjust her life and follow me.

I said, "Babe, I'm quitting my job (which is always a good way to start out). We are going to raise support, join The Traveling Team, say goodbye to our house and our friends and family and travel ten months of the year in a van, mobilizing thousands of students to catch this vision for the world and join in God's Great Commission."

She blinked twice and said, "OK."

The reason she could say yes to the second question is that she had already said yes to the first. That is what she "signed up" for. Now, the other reason she said "yes" is the fact that my wife is a studlier Christian than me and she had already decided she was ready to invest her life in the Great Commission. But the central idea is the same—lordship. The lordship of Jesus is central to our involvement in His task to reach the world. It is not optional. If you said yes to following Him, He is not asking you whether or not you feel like joining Him in the Great Commission. That is where He is headed. You must decide to either allow Him to interrupt the course of your life, adjust and align yourself with His agenda, or live life in the outer courts of what He is doing.

God has purchased us. When I was younger and one of my friends wanted a bike and their parents couldn't afford it, they would go to Wal–Mart, put down some money as a deposit and put the bike on layaway. It meant that the deposit was secure; in the end you would get the bike. Until then, Wal–Mart could still do whatever they wanted with the bike. They owned it. Many people seem to have this view of their salvation. God, however, did not put us on layaway. He has purchased us. It isn't that He just put down a deposit and wants you in Heaven in the end—He bought you. When the Father purchased you, He brought you home to His Son and now the Son has full ownership of you. He can steer you wherever He wishes. That is what it means to be under the lordship of the King.

living and loving

When I started dating Rebecca, I noticed that I started going places and doing things that I had never done before. Movies like Sleepless in Seattle started making it on the regular rotation. I thought Bath and Body Works sold plumbing supplies. But now I know my wife well enough to know what her heart delights in. And I have found that I get the greatest joy out of seeing her enjoy the things that bring her heart joy. I delight in the things she delights in. When you fall in love with someone, you begin to love the things that they love. Do you know God well enough to know what you might do with your life that would bring His heart joy? Do you see His heart for the world? The more we do and the more we grow in our love for God, the more we begin to love the things God loves—the nations. This may be comforting if you are like me and don't get all choked up about people in poverty you see on TV, or people in China that you have never seen. I used to think I must be the most cold–hearted person on the planet. The issue was not about this horizontal love for people, as much as it is about this vertical love for God and the things that God loves—those people. As I have grown in seeing God's heart in His Word and grown in loving Him more, I have begun to care more about the world. To live life by the compass means you allow God to direct the affections of your heart toward the North Star of His heart—His glory made known in all the earth.

God is not your co-pilot

> "It is possible to deceive ourselves into thinking that we have biblical passions when, in reality, all we have done is baptize the values of our culture and given them Christian names."– Floyd McClung

Your life is a gift to God for the enjoyment of His heart. When guys get married there is this temptation for them to take the toys that they want for themselves and disguise them as gifts for their wives. Guys are smooth at it—big screen TV, PlayStation, and the new SUV "family car" for her safety. There was a Simpson's episode where Homer bought Marge a bowling ball for her birthday.

As it falls out of the box and smashes the birthday cake, Marge replies, "Homer! You didn't buy that bowling ball for me, you bought it for yourself!"

Homer quickly argues, "No, I didn't. But … if you don't want it, I know someone who does."

Marge fumes on, and finally Homer says, "Fine, I'll take it back."

Marge yells, "You can't take it back—you had your name engraved in it!"

Christians are just more subtle than Homer. I had a student come up to me after a missions talk I gave and basically gave me the same spiel. He was an artist and he wanted to move to Europe to begin an art studio of all his paintings. He told me about how when he becomes successful and famous, people will begin to buy his paintings for thousands of dollars. Once that happened (here's where it gets good) he was going to use the money to fund missions trips for himself and others. "Great huh," he kind of nods like I'm going to just hug him for being so missions-minded. I gently put my arm around him and said, "Doug, that's an awesome idea, but did you notice that your plan for God hinges on you becoming a famous artist? Is that God's dream for your life, or is it really just yours?"

It is like Christians want to take their former life pursuits and wrap them in a nice Christian-looking package with an "it's my ministry" bow on top and everything's cool, right? God is not fooled. I don't think God is impressed by you slapping an icthus on the back of your agenda and asking Him to bless it. He is asking you to give Him the things that He wants and live for His dreams, not ours. God is not "your co–pilot" as if you and Jesus are in the front seat—you're steering while He is riding shotgun sipping on a mocha Frappuccino and making suggestions. That's what my pastor calls bumper sticker theology. The reality is that King Jesus is driving this thing, you aren't shotgun, you aren't a backseat driver, you aren't even in the trunk. You are more like a water skier, towed wherever the driver wishes. If you want to follow Him all you have to do is hang on for the ride. Otherwise you can let go and drift. There is only room in this missionary family for one purpose. Jesus only had room for one agenda in His life. This is how He got it. *"The Son can do nothing of Himself, but He can only do what He sees the Father doing."* Jesus lived by the North Star of what He saw God doing. He lived life on purpose.

CHAPTER FIFTEEN

Tools for the Journey

"World Christians are day–to–day disciples for whom Christ's global cause has become the integrating, overriding priority for all that life is for them."

– David Bryant

five habits – the tools for the journey

When you begin to join God on the journey and follow His heart for the nations, there are some habits that will begin to show up in your life. God gives us these skills as our tools for the journey. Each of us has been given spiritual gifts and habits for the sake of the journey ahead, not only for us, but also for the success of the one mission. I am going to describe five of these habits. I call them habits because they are learned behavior. All are available and all should proactively be put into practice. If you begin to think of them as roles or callings, you get the idea that some people have one role and other people have another. That thinking leads to the idea that if you are active in one, it somehow excuses you from the other four. They are habits for every Christian. You may major in one and minor in the others in this season in your life, but someone who is truly on the journey will be working to grow in all five. Learn them, pack them for the journey, and let the compass direct you in using each one.

ropes - the habit of sending others

"How then will they call on Him in whom they have not believed? How will they believe in Him whom they have not heard? And how will they hear without a preacher? How will they preach <u>unless they are sent</u>" (Romans 10:14–15)?

One of the most memorable Tom Cruise moments is as Ethan Hunt in Mission Impossible, dangling from the cable held from above, only inches from the pressure sensitive floor of the interior computer room of the CIA. Tom wasn't alone. It took the whole team. You can't have Tom Cruise without a crazy Russian holding the cable and a computer nerd outside in the van. They were "senders." James Bond always gets hooked up with all his gadgets before he goes off to save the world. Q, in a way, is a "sender."

You may not be the person to pack up and move to Kyrgyzstan, or Iraq, or Indonesia, but God may have another vital purpose for your life as you yield to His journey. The *ropes* you carry are to lower another teammate into the battle. You may practice the habit of becoming a strong sender, and "holding the ropes" for someone that goes cross–culturally. The person living their life by the compass uses their money strategically to bring about the greatest advancement in the Great Commission. They are living a simple lifestyle in order to free up resources, and then using those resources in the places that further the gospel on to its destination. This is what Ralph Winter calls living a "Wartime Lifestyle." Serving as a sender does not just mean you save money and live simply. Sometime in wartime it is necessary to spend great amounts on equipment and men in order to win the war. In the military, for every frontline soldier you see fighting, there are dozens of support personnel working behind the scenes to keep him out there. They are taking care of his food rations, his equipment, and all the logistics so that he can concentrate on the battle. The kingdom of God is no different. For every frontline missionary, there are hundreds of world Christians, living their lives by the compass, but serving behind the scenes by financially supporting or helping to serve the person working cross–culturally. I know a couple in Los Angeles, Wendy and Scott that are holding the ropes for others. She and her husband both work and serve as purposeful, committed senders. They have decided to live off his salary and give her entire salary away to missions work. They are making a deep impact on the world, living life on purpose, but they never leave Pasadena. Living for God's purpose in the world is not an issue of just location, but lordship and lifestyle. In this habit, the compass directs your finances and lifestyle choices.

walkie talkie - the habit of praying for the world

"The person who mobilizes the church to pray will make the largest contribution in history to world evangelization."
– Andrew Murray

When you think of prayer, do you think of the one–way "domestic intercom" as one author calls it, where we tell God the list of stuff we need like a drive–thru at McDonalds? The walkie talkie is the two–way communicator with the commander, the head scout of the journey. Its purpose is not only to ask him for supplies for the journey, but to allow him to communicate to us about the needs along the way.

Generally speaking, each time Jesus sent out His desiples to the nations He would charge them to pray for one thing. He was with the disciples and as He looked on the crowds of people, He felt compassion. Then He turned to the disciples saying, *"The harvest is plentiful, but the workers are few. Therefore ask the Lord of the harvest to send out workers into His harvest"* (Matthew 9:37–38). The compass directed Jesus' prayers and He has commanded us, His future disciples, to pray in the same way.

Maybe you can't relate, but I stink at prayer. I would love to pretend that I just wake up and pray for hours every day, but I don't. In fact, I need to have a structured plan if I am going to pray for the world. The reason most people don't pray is not that they don't want to; it is just that they don't plan to. The difficult thing about beginning a habit of prayer is starting a plan. The difficult thing about continuing a habit of prayer is not running out of things to pray for. There is a limitless amount of things going on in the world right now that need prayer. The problem is that I don't know 99.9% of them. We need to open a door for information about the needs in the world to flow consistently into our life so that we can have a steady diet of things to pray for. Information is like the food that a Christian needs to have a healthy prayer life. If you are starved for information your prayer life will look sickly and weak. It is a win/win. They need the prayer, we need to pray. Begin to gather resources like the book *Operation World*, or utilize websites that profile people groups or world news. Prayer is the work of missions. The person who goes only reaps the fruit of the faithful prayers of World Christians.

bifocal glasses - the habit of welcoming internationals

"So show your love for the alien, for you were aliens in the land of Egypt" (Deuteronomy 10:19).

At one of the larger universities we visited, Rebecca met with a girl to talk about world missions. As they talked the girl obviously had a heart for China. She wanted to go to China. She said she was called to China. She wanted to learn Chinese and it was all that she could do to not quit school right then and go to China. Finally Rebecca asked her, "Well, are there any Chinese students here at your campus?"

The girl looked back at her, kind of confused, then responded, "Well, yeah, but they kind of cluster. They cluster together and they all live in one dorm."

Rebecca pursues, "Well, have you ever been to the Chinese dorm?"

"No," she replies, "It's all the way on the other side of campus. And they all just stay to themselves!"

Finally Rebecca points out the obvious, "Tonya, what makes you think you are going to cross an ocean and reach out to Chinese people, if you won't even cross the campus to reach out to them."

"If you have run with footmen and they have tired you out, then how can you compete with horses? If you fall down in a land of peace, how will you do in the thicket of the Jordan" (Jeremiah 12:5)? In the original Hebrew it translates like this, "Hey tough guy, if you can't hack it when it's safe and easy, don't even think about running with the big dogs." God has organized it where the nations have come to us in many ways. The first step for you on the journey may be to begin reaching out to the internationals around you. After all, if you aren't sharing your faith when it's comfortable, what makes you think you will be able to do it when it's not?

The Old Testament contains over forty references to looking out for the "alien" or foreigner among you. God is always moving people to the places where they can meet him or make him known. If God has brought internationals into your community, it is serious business of Heaven. There are 740,000 international students storming the universities of the U.S. and 95% of them will go all four years and never be invited into an American home.[1] Millions of internationals from restricted access countries and difficult nations to reach are coming right to the neighborhoods of America. There are 173 languages spoken in the Los Angeles school system alone. The question is do we "see" them? I went through most of college with a sort of "people blindness."

Jesus didn't have people blindness. God had organized it that Jesus could share the gospel with Gentiles and model reaching out to internationals for the disciples. He reaches out to the two demon possessed men of Gadarenes (Matthew 8:28), heals the Centurion's servant (Matthew 8:5–11), feeds the four thousand Gentiles (Matthew 15), heals the Canaanite's daughter (Matthew 15:21–28), touches the demon–possessed man in Gerasene (Mark 5) and has a long spiritual conversation with the Samaritan woman at the well (John 4). Two–thirds of Jesus' major miracles are done toward internationals, Gentiles, not His own people.

We need this "bifocal" vision of being able to see the nations of the world, while at the same time, seeing and reaching out to the nations right in front of us. International students are incredibly strategic. They will likely become the future leaders either here in America or back in their home countries. At the turn of the century, forty–five percent of the world's leaders had once studied at American universities. Some people on the journey will take opportunities to plant themselves at the crossroads and impact the travelers that come by. You can make a powerful impact on the nations by starting with the nations around you. Dorothy didn't have to leave Kansas to find what she was looking for, it was all around her. Sometimes in the journey—there's no place like home.

boots - the habit of going cross-cultural

"With these facts before you and with the command of the Lord Jesus to go and preach the gospel to every creature, the burden of proof will lie on you to show by what circumstances you were meant to stay out of the foreign mission field."– Hudson Taylor

If you are going to walk the journey, you must be open to the option of going long–term. The command has been for us to "go." The facts in the world demand that someone must stand in the gap. Obviously, if the journey is going to be completed, it will hinge on an army of relentless, passionate goers. Plan on going and be willing to stay if God directs you to. The way to find your specific niche in the journey and exactly where God's purpose is for your life is to obey and see. God clarifies in the midst of obedience. The answers to the journey lie in obedience to the revelation we already have. *"Your ears will hear a word behind you, 'This is the way, walk in it,' whenever you turn to the right or to the left" (Isaiah 30:21).* The idea is that we are already walking in obedience when we hear His direction more clearly. God can't steer a parked car. As we obey His clear command to "go therefore and make disciples of all nations," He is able to "steer" us and guide us because we have proven ourselves faithful. He is not going to throw His pearls, or guidance, to the swine that are unwilling to move forward in obedience in what He is clear about. Don't assume that your life's mission is to just live in suburbia and give money. Any of the other habits can be done on the mission field as well as here. Keith Green would say, "You should never have to worry about there not being enough Christians staying home to support missionaries. There will always be enough people around who will not answer the call to go—who will stay home and gladly just send a check (instead of themselves) to reach the lost. After all, nothing is easier to give than money (except nothing)."

Everyone can go short–term. The person on the journey knows that they need to have a habit of getting cross–cultural once in a while, in order to sharpen their vision and receive new direction from the Lord. Going is the habit that sharpens the saw. It makes us into better welcomers because we know what it feels like to be an international. It helps us in the habit of prayer because we have been there and seen the needs first–hand. It deepens our commitment to giving because we realize the money involved in going and the needs on the field. We live in an American un–reality, the Disneyland of the universe. It is good for us just to "step out of the matrix" for a little while and see what reality is like for the rest of humanity.

I have a friend, Brad, who grew up in San Diego. He was a pro surfer in high school and had plenty going for him. Then, through his youth minister, he caught a vision for what God was doing. Soon, Brad allowed God to radically interrupt the course of his life. At 18, he left to train with New Tribes Mission and within a few years he was in Papua New Guinea, living among an unreached people group called the Iteri. Brad gave twenty years of his life to the Iteri tribe; he translated the Bible into their language, planted a church, and raised a family. Brad is such a normal guy. He would surf on the weekends; he even had some bags of concrete flown in so he could build a basketball court for his boys. But Brad lived his life by the compass and made his life count. After finishing the work there, he came back to San Diego for a two–year furlough. Then the neighboring villages began to write letters to him. Brad, with tears in his eyes, shared these letters with me and a small group of students. This is one.

Wapia Sainaki
Sinou Village
Sandaun Province

"What's going on? Where is our help? Have you for got about us? We of Sinou haven't forgot about wanting a missionary, we carry a huge heavy constantly about this.

We carry this heavy cause we fear for our lives. We know the paipel (Bible) says you should come and tell us. Us dark ones need it..how will we go to God's place if not? Only those who know will go, how will we know if no one teaches us?

That's my worry, we want a missionary now to give us God's talk."

Brad is in San Diego with plans to take his family to another unreached people in a restricted country soon. He is only in his forties. The last time I saw him he had just cut his nose that week wakeboarding. Brad has made a contribution with his life to the Great Commission that will never be taken away. He's not more spiritual than the rest. He has caught a vision for the North Star and is ruined for anything less than the journey he was created for. Brad lives life by the compass because that is where he fits. Jesus also allowed the compass to direct His location. *"I must preach the kingdom of God to the other cities also, for I was sent for this purpose"* (Luke 4:42–43). When we are on the journey the compass directs our feet—where we choose to live. God wants to use you to bring one of these peoples and nations to the throne as your contribution to the worship of Heaven. Will you allow the gospel to radically interrupt the course of your life? Is it worth it? Ask Brad.

lantern – the habit of mobilizing

As you follow the compass, you naturally gather others to travel the road with you. Your obedience in yielding your life to the North Star is a lantern—lighting the way for others to the source of life's greatest rewards. Everybody wants to follow someone that is going somewhere with a purpose. Remember Forrest Gump's run across America and back? It was hardly a noble cause, he "just felt like running." Even so, others ran just to see what made him tick. They were inspired. Forrest was a mobilizer. Everyone mobilizes to something. I could spend some time with you and figure out pretty quickly what your "thing" is. *"Out of the overflow of the heart the mouth speaks" (Matthew 12:34).* That's all a mobilizer does. He allows the things that are on God's heart to burn so brightly in his heart that it begins to come out in his speech and overflow onto others. He is active in educating, networking, organizing and rallying people to the journey for the sake of the nations.

Imagine if you were standing on the beach, and just off the shore, you saw a ship full of people that was sinking. The people were drowning and you had to act quickly. You could either dive in and rescue maybe one or two people, or you could turn and awaken the hundred sleeping lifeguards behind you, rallying others to the task. The person following the journey to its destination knows that it will take more than just himself to complete the task. He will need to mobilize as many committed World Christians to going, sending, praying and welcoming as he can. The resources of the church are incredible. There are 600 churches and 460,000 Christians for every one unreached people group.

The mobilizer is trying to tap into the resources and hearts of the church for the cause of the Great Commission. You might say that the potential laborers are plentiful but the mobilizers are few. Every Christian is a part of this missionary family with a responsibility to pass the blessing of the gospel on to the ends of the earth. We don't have to worry about whether or not we are supposed to be involved—we are all called. We just need to get mobilized.

Phil Parshall, missionary, author, and mobilizer, said it this way, *"Someone must sound the rallying call. Those who desire to see others trained, prepared and released to ministry are known as mobilizers. Mobilizers stir other Christians to active concern for reaching the world. They coordinate efforts between senders, the local churches, sending agencies, and missionaries on the field. Mobilizers are essential. To understand the role of mobilizers, think of World War II as a parallel. Only 10% of the American population went to the war. Of those, only 1% were actually on the firing lines. However, for them to be successful in their mission, the entire country had to be mobilized!"*

Wesley Tullis, formerly a Director of Prayer Mobilization for YWAM states: *"Essentially mobilization refers to any process by which God's people are awakened and kept moving and growing until they find their place for strategic involvement in the task of completing world evangelization. Mobilizers are those who channel key resources, training, and vision for world evangelization to the Body of Christ."*

Our job is to free up resources and people from the excuses that keep them sidelined. These excuses are hurdles preventing the gospel of salvation from going out to the people for which Christ died. 2 Corinthians 10:5 says, *"We are destroying speculations and every lofty thing raised up against the knowledge of God ..."* These "speculations and ideas" come in many clever and intimidating forms, and at times appear so "lofty" that they paralyze a person from even trying. That is the job description of the missions mobilizer—to free people to join the journey.

Dorothy, in *The Wizard of Oz*, rallied people to her journey to see the wizard. Sometimes it was just because of the enthusiasm and hope that she had in the reward ahead that caused the strange band from Oz to join her. But each of them had to be mobilized. Dorothy had to unhook the Scarecrow and oil the Tin Man. Sometimes God will call you to hit the Cowardly Lion in the face, but you might just mobilize him in the process. No one wants to have their life interrupted, not even by the gospel. You must find words that shock people out of their love affair with the world. Your job is to call people to obey the lordship of Jesus and their responsibility in His mission. As you follow the compass, you gather others to travel the road with you.

---

1. ISI International, www.isionline.org.

CHAPTER SIXTEEN

Looking Back

But Jesus said to him, "No one, after putting his hand to the plow and looking back, is fit for the kingdom of God."

– Luke 9:62

bound homeward

The main reason some people will never finish the journey, or never even begin, is that they cannot let go of the safety and security of the present. It is almost as if the more God blesses us, the more we have to lose. We cling. We get consumed with our stuff. While I was writing this book, a couple in our church lost their home. While they were away for the weekend, a thunderstorm came through and their house was struck by lightning. It caught on fire and began to burn. The neighbors called the fire department, but the fire trucks couldn't get there because of a huge tree that had fallen across the road. Almost like Job, in one night due to strange circumstances, they lost everything. My wife and I had them over for dinner later that month and they were discussing what freedom they had found in losing all they had collected. It was funny, but people thought they were serving them by offering some of their extra junk to them. They were being given CDs, pictures, clothes, stereos, but in the process they realized that they didn't want those things again. The husband basically said to me, "You know, it is amazing how much of our lives revolve around our stuff. We work to collect our stuff. We work to maintain our stuff. We clean it, straighten it, replace it, fix it, upgrade it, look at it, and sometimes use it. But there is great freedom when you are released from the treadmill of possessions." They are not looking back. In fact, this couple has taken the event as a signpost on the journey, that God may want them to redirect their lives to the foreign mission field. Is this event a tragedy? From God's perspective and theirs—no. They are allowing God to speak through a lightning storm and interrupt the course of their life. They were not looking backward to the home here, but forward to the reward of a heavenly city. "For we know that if the earthly tent which is our house is torn down, we have a building from God, a house not made with hands, eternal in the heavens" (2 Corinthians 5:1).

the un-sacrifice

> The great danger is not that we will renounce our faith, but settle for a mediocre version of it.– John Ortberg

We look back because deep down we are afraid that we are missing out on something if we decide to follow God and live for His purpose. It's like the guy who wants to get married but keep all his old girlfriends too. We trust God to provide for our salvation and say we give our lives to Him, but we are not sure if He can be trusted to meet our needs. Ultimately we decide we should fend for ourselves in that area. Even the language of our church suggests that people who devote their lives to the Great Commission "sacrifice so much" for His kingdom work. We were created for the journey. We are a kingdom of priests and a part of the missionary family that God has given the privilege of reaching the world for Him. This is our designed destiny, it's where we fit. Our involvement in God's global purpose is for the triumph of His glory among the nations, our joy as we find our purpose in His design, and for the eternal completion of the worship mosaic in Heaven: something that will last for all eternity. Can we now call it a sacrifice? C.T. Studd said, *"If Christ be God and died for me, there is no sacrifice that I could make for Him that is too great."* It is no sacrifice. A sacrifice implies that what is given up is of greater value than what is gained. In this case, what is given up is the temporary, false, perishing, ultimately unsatisfying, lesser version of pleasure that the world offers. In contrast, what is gained is the ever satisfying, God–exalting, eternal, purpose filled, joy saturated life that is truly life. It is no sacrifice to give up what is worthless to gain what is priceless. The idea of sacrifice is not just about our gain or loss, but also communicates our view of the worthiness of God. A sacrifice is only as noble as the cause behind the sacrifice is worthy. If God and His glory are infinitely worthy then there is no sacrifice too great. No sacrifice too great means just that—no sacrifice. If we are to fulfill the Great Commission we must be willing to "love not our lives even unto death." The gospel has the authority to interrupt our lives, moving us to a new position, sometimes toward risk and danger, in order that the gospel might be passed on through us to the nations. We must count the cost and move radically forward for the sake of the journey. The compass always points true north. It doesn't stop to ask whether it will be safe or easy. It is only when our lives are interconnected to the broader story that death can gain both meaning and purpose.

watching your back

Somehow we have the ability to disconnect ourselves from reality in order to avoid risk. Like Cypher in The Matrix, the thing that drove him to sell out his friends was a desire to have his memory erased and go back to life in the computer–generated world. Some people would rather live in the illusion, eat steak and forget reality on planet earth. There is a shortage of noble men and women—of heroes. Our thought is that in today's times the Good Samaritan would have probably gotten sued by the guy he was trying to help, or at least gotten a disease. He should have just offered to call 911, or turned the other way.

We will do almost anything besides get directly involved. While we were at a school up north, right after the September 11th attacks, I picked up a university newspaper. There was an article about a survey done at Harvard. Students were asked whether or not they favored military action against those that attacked America. That was a big question in the news at the time. It was no surprise that 68% of the students said that the favored military action against the terrorists who were behind the attack. But the article was about another discovery. A follow up question asked if that student was willing to join the fight personally. 38% of the students who said they favored military action also admitted that they were unwilling to take part in military action themselves. The author went on to say, *"One has to worry about students who would favor military action only as long as they can sit comfortably in Cambridge."*[1] The author has it right. Even the lost world sees an inconsistency in our message and in our lives. Kevin Turner says that, *"The world isn't looking for a better sermon on love; they are looking for a better demonstration of it."* Months before 9–11 there was an outbreak of shark attacks in Florida. In more than one case there were reports of lifeguards that stood on the shore and watched as children were being attacked. They stood and did nothing—except look out for number one. Has our failure to join God in His mission of world–wide redemption also been the cause of some of our local failure to win the communities we live in? A gospel that is not worth suffering for and proclaiming is no true gospel. There is no power in a church full of draft dodgers—watching their backs and dodging the responsibility of the Great Commission. As the author of the article ended, *"We must answer the calling of our time—for if we don't, who will?"*

> *"Deliver those who are being taken away to death, and those who are staggering to slaughter, oh hold them back. If you say, 'See, we did not know this,' does He not consider it who weighs the hearts? And does He not know it who keeps your soul? And will He not render to man according to his work"* (Proverbs 24:11–12)?

looking for something

> *"Tell the students to give up their small ambitions and come eastward to preach the gospel of Christ."*– Francis Xavier

I live by the assumption that behind it all, no person really wants to waste his or her life. All of us are looking for our purpose and our calling. Our quest for meaning is like the "merchant seeking fine pearls." He finds the pearl of great price—but only because he is "seeking." The answer in finding the life we are seeking is truly in losing the life we are holding onto. He who wants to save his life to use toward the eternal will have to be okay with losing at life in the things that are temporary.

When we were at the University of South Carolina, I met with a student named Nathan. We sat down, Nathan wrote down his email for me and it was CEO@... something. I looked at this freshman, and said, "CEO? Is that your dad's email?" He went on to tell me that he was the CEO of a company that he started in high school. He sold print cartridges on the internet. I thought to myself, "Who is this, Doogie Howser?" There aren't many freshmen out there who have their own companies. Nathan began to tell me that he was thinking about going overseas, in fact he had started to fill out an application, but then he got scared.

He said, "I thought, wait a minute ... If I go overseas, what is going to happen to my company? I have worked hard to build it."

Finally, after discussing it some more, I asked Nathan, "Can I tell you something?"

"Sure."

"Nathan, there's always going to be somebody to sell print cartridges on eBay. Why don't you give your life to the things that other people can't and won't do?"

Nathan left that day and I didn't hear from him until a month later. He emailed me out of the blue and said, "Claude, I've thought about what you said, and I decided to spend no less than two months overseas this summer. I'm just going!" At the end of the email I found out how Nathan paid for his trip—he sold his company. He had found a greater passion. Nathan allowed the gospel to interrupt the course of his life in order to live for a purpose that was bigger than himself and a cause great enough to "sacrifice" for. I still talk to Nathan today and if you ask him—it was no sacrifice.

This generation is looking for a cause to live for. If you give them a cause to live for they will lay their life down for it. Samuel Zwemer would challenge students saying, *"Don't make a living—make a life!"* Jesus died, not for the sanctified American Dream or to just bring us to Heaven, but to bring us into the cause of His Father. He died to connect our lives into a story that was bigger than just us. *"And He died for all, so that they who live might no longer live for themselves, but for Him who died and rose again on their behalf"* (2 Corinthians 5:15). Christ died to rescue you from living for small things and making small plans. You can either get your direction from His North Star or choose to ruin your life. The scary thing is that if you choose to walk your own journey, God will allow it, even though you waste your life.

making your own light

> *"Woe to those who deeply hide their plans from the Lord, and whose deeds are done in a dark place, and they say, 'Who sees us?' or 'Who knows us'"(Isaiah 29:15)?*

All of us desire to make a difference for eternal things, things that will last. Your desire to have meaning and God's desire to use you in His plans of world–wide redemption are reconciled into one passion. They are made to be united in one. However, God is perfectly willing to let you ruin your life. He will offer nothing more than His Word, which is saturated with the language of the reward found in loving Him and aligning our lives with His agenda. God is trying to help us see beyond the illusion of the glitter that the world bombards us with to see that the true gold and silver are found on the narrow path. God warns us about living for our plans instead of His. In Isaiah 50 there is a description of two types of people looking for direction: those that walk in the darkness and those that make their own light.

> *"Who is among you that fears the Lord, that obeys the voice of His servant, that walks in darkness and has no light? Let him trust in the name of the Lord and rely on his God"* (Isaiah 50:10).

We would usually associate "walking in darkness" with being lost and in rebellion against God, but in this case it is the picture of complete dependence on Him. Picture a person walking through a dark forest. The darkness forces us to trust and rely on our God. There is a kind of inner peace found in this life. We trust that God is completely sovereign and causes everything to work together for the good of those that faithfully follow His voice in the darkness. We can walk securely—not because there aren't dangers in the woods, but because the voice guiding us has a perfect plan. The voice of God IS the light of our path, revealing our direction and our North Star in His written word. *"Your word is a lamp to my feet and a light to my path"* (Psalms 119:105). The alternative is to either grope around in our own stubbornness or even worse—to manufacture our own light. Is it sin to be a Christian and live a life centered around your agenda? Here is God's answer.

> *"Behold, all you who kindle a fire, who encircle yourselves with firebrands, walk in the light of your fire and among the brands you have set ablaze. This you will have from My hand: You will lie down in torment"* (Isaiah 50:11).

The person who walks by the light he has made walks in constant fear, saying in his heart, "God cannot be trusted to know what is best for me. He doesn't know the dangers of where He is calling me." This man is paranoid—living in the fear of the very shadows his light creates. When he lies down to sleep, he cannot because he must keep one eye open to watch for danger. He lies down in torment because of his fear and need to protect himself in life. Who is sovereign in this way of doing life? Man is. I must make my own light. I will navigate this life. I will choose the safe path.

Here's what really worries me about this picture. If you want to live by your own North Star, God will not strike you down. However, when you have spent your life on all the things you thought would make you happy, the nice house, the car, the clothes, and the life of comfort, the emptiness will still remain. As you lie down in your bed at night, alone with your thoughts of what you have exchanged your life for, a lullaby of regrets will ring in your ears, whispering, "You settled for the outer courts, the illusion of the glitter." That is what it looks like to lie down in torment. The highest bracket for suicide is not teenagers. It is adults in the first year after retirement. They have finished investing their lives. They have traveled to the end of their journey and many find it was the wrong North Star they were following. Three–hundred and sixty–five days of lying down in torment is too much for them. If you want to save your life—lose it on the things that matter. Lose your life with all your might.

> *"And people who do not know the Lord ask why in the world we waste our lives as missionaries. They forget that they too are expending their lives... and when the bubble has burst, they will have nothing of eternal significance to show for the years they have wasted."*
>
> *– Nate Saint.*

---

1. Herbert London, *Blaming America Still Dominant on U.S. Cam puses*, The Northern Iowan, p9

CHAPTER SEVENTEEN

Looking Forward

forward motives

There are many motivations for becoming involved in God's heart for the world. Some are worried that they have bad motives. When we are sincerely seeking God's desires, bad motives are rare. The Lord promises that as we delight ourselves in Him He will give us the desires of our heart. What I have found is that He doesn't mean that He will give you some wish list of desires that you have been hoping for. Instead He will give you new desires—His desires. As you delight in and love the Lord, you will begin to love the things that He loves—all the nations. You may find that you are excited about a specific people group or a particular country. God may be welling up inside of you a deep desire to be a strong, faithful sender and World Christian to the glory of God. The reality is that there are many great motives, and you may just not find yourself motivated by the ones you were told were the "good ones." Jesus used several motivations for missions when challenging His disciples to join in the journey of reaching the world. Some are motivated by the need (Matthew 9:37). You may be moved by the sheer facts over the disproportion of laborers and the 2.4 billion people that are separated from the gospel right now. You may be motivated to follow Jesus out of obedience to His lordship in your life (Matthew 28:18—20). Jesus used guilt at times (Acts 20:26, Ezekiel 33:6), reminding us that we will be held accountable, as the watchmen, for the blood of those who are not warned. You may be motivated by love. Jesus himself was motivated by compassion at times (Matthew 9:36, Mark 1:41). You may have a firm concept of the reality of Hell and the destiny of the lost (Luke 12:5, Romans 3:18, Matthew 13:41–42). You may be motivated by the forward thinking of a life lived for the future glory and reward that awaits us with our King (Luke 18:29–30). You may find that joining the journey is where life truly has purpose (Matthew 16:26–27, I Peter 1:24). Finally, you may have a God—centered passion for God's glory to be made known in all the earth (John 15:8, John 17:4).

Which one is the *right* motivation? None of them! That's because they are *all* great motivations. I believe that at most, they are just progressions. We may jump on the path at different points, but in the end we are all laboring for the same North Star and the same destination. You may jump on at hearing the facts or out of love, while I may resolve to just obey despite my heart, praying for it to change as I move forward. Ultimately with time, I hope to say that I am on the journey for the same motivation that God has—for His glory. You may be there already. God doesn't require a perfect heart to start the journey—just a heart that is willing to be molded along the way.

forward thinking

"And without faith it is impossible to please Him, for he who comes to God must believe that <u>He is</u> and that <u>He is a rewarder</u> of those who seek Him" (Hebrews 11:6).

This verse holds a forward thinking key to anchoring our feet to the journey. There seems to be a connection here that is missing from much of the Church, as well as from my life. In order to please God, what He requires is faith. Not just faith in any god, but faith in the true God. The faith described in this verse has two strong legs that it stands on. One leg is the strong faith that "He is"; that God exists. He is real. God is, and there is no other besides Him. The second leg of faith grounds us firmly alongside the first truth. This God who does certainly exist "is a rewarder." That is who He is: a rewarder. He is, and He rewards. His rewards are not necessarily in this life. As you read on, you will find in Hebrews 11 that many of the heroes of the faith looked forward to the reward, but did not receive it here on earth. They were living for a heavenly city, a future hope of glory. They were forward thinking, setting their minds on the future reward. Moses considered the reproach of Christ greater riches than the treasures of Egypt; for he was looking forward to the reward. Moses believed God existed, he spoke to Him and saw Him, and the evidence of his faith was a life lived for God the rewarder.

The question is: Can someone claim to believe in their heart that God is, and live as though He is not a rewarder? Let me put it another way. Can I proclaim that "He is" and that I am living for God's reward, but build my own treasure here, just in case "He is not?" Is my faith in the true God, the One who is and who is a rewarder? They cannot be separated in God's being, how can they be separated in my living? Does my real reward come from Best Buy (just insert your store here with mine)? The world mocks Christianity because they see clearly what we refuse to acknowledge— the beam of the American Dream in our eye as we claim to live for the eternal. Our joy must be anchored in Heaven. God's treasure is greater and more lasting. It is as true as God's existence is true. *"Whom have I in Heaven but You? And besides You, I desire nothing on earth"* (Psalms 73:25). I picture an archer, pulling back the arrow, with his eyes fixed in a distant gaze. We must live a life for Jesus, with a vision that is fixed up and over, past the ill—treatment, past the pleasures of sin, past the treasures of this world to the treasure that is true and truly satisfying. Then our lives would send a message to the world that our happiness is not wrapped up in material or temporal things. We live for a God who is real. His reward is real. Live life in this reality, and the watching world will beg to know this Jesus we love and this hope we stand so firmly on. *"Instruct them to do good, to be rich in good works, to be generous and ready to share, storing up for themselves the treasure of a good foundation for the future, so that they may take hold of the life which is truly life"* (1 Timothy 6:18–19).

forward moving

A pastor tells the story about counseling a friend through choosing a life direction. Most of the people I interact with fall so perfectly into this situation that I had to include his simple, but profound answer. Here is the story.

"His dilemma was that there were so many good options that it was hard to know which one to take.

His greatest concern was doing something that would go against God's will for his life. He waited with earnestness for God to speak to him in a clear and undeniable way, but nothing seemed to come. The more there was silence, the more he was filled with uncertainty. For some reason, he did not feel he had permission to choose, so he chose not to choose. And so, by not choosing, he was essentially choosing to do nothing.

I gave him the same advice that I have given many others who seemed destined to pitch a tent at the crossroad. I told him, '*Just do something.*'

He seemed shocked at what seemed a callous disregard for the will of God. He responded that he had too much respect for the sovereignty of God to just do something.

I asked him if he thought that Hitler and Stalin had been capable of thwarting the sovereignty of God.

He said, '*Of course not.*'

I pointed out that if men and women who gave their lives for a purpose counter to the will of God could not stop God's purpose in history, how could someone who longs to do God's will and chooses to do something in line with God's character? I told him I had too much respect for the sovereignty of God to think that he or I could mess it up."[1]

"But the noble man makes noble plans; and by noble plans he stands" (Isaiah 32:8). You were created to do something—to walk the journey that God has created you for. There are far too many sidelined Christians, waiting for God to put them in the game. Everyone God calls to himself, He enlists in His work. All we have to do is begin to walk the journey. "*Your*

ears will hear a word behind you, 'This is the way, walk in it,'
whenever you turn to the right or to the left" (Isaiah 30:21).
Move forward and He will guide your steps. A great life is
not made up in the amount of minutes, but what is done
with them. Do something great by looking forward to the
reward and living life by the compass.

forward living

> *"Radical decisions, choices and lifestyles are the founding*
> *fathers of my life. Can I now waiver?"– John R. Mott*

At 3:15 a.m., on the night of March 13, 1964, Katherine Genovese[2] was returning home from her job at a bar in
Queens. Genovese parked her car in a lot next to her apartment building, locked her car and began the 100–foot walk
to her apartment, not realizing that she had been spotted
leaving the bar and followed. Soon, though, she noticed a
man at the far end of the parking lot and changed direction.
She got only as far as a street light when the man grabbed
her. "Oh my God, he stabbed me! Please help me! Please
help me!" she screamed. Lights went on in a nearby 10–story
apartment house. The assailant walked to a car and drove
off. Genovese struggled to her feet. The apartment building's
lights went out. Then the man came back and stabbed her
again. "I'm dying," she shrieked, "I'm dying!" Again, lights
went on. Again, the man went to his car and drove away.
Genovese struggled to her feet, but the assailant returned
a third time. By then, she had crawled to her apartment
building. The man stabbed her a third time and Katherine
Genovese died. Finally, at 3:50 A.M., the police received a
phone call from a neighbor of Genovese's. In two minutes
they were on the scene. The police and all of America were
shocked to discover that there were 38 eye witnesses to

Katherine's murder. What was most shocking was that out of all 38, not one called the police, went down to help or did anything to prevent her murder that night. Now the story is taught in Psychology 101 and is given the term "bystander apathy." The idea is that there is a diffusion of responsibility among a group of people, where each assumes that someone else will act. Each eyewitness that night somehow went back to sleep with the calm assurance that someone else would go down to assist her, and that someone else would call the police. But the reality was that the "someone else" was thinking the same thing.

Whatever you do—you must do something. James 4:17 says, *"Therefore, to one who knows the right thing to do and does not do it, to him it is sin."* Have you taken personal responsibility for the Great Commission? We may think that we have nothing to offer or that we are unprepared to get involved and make a difference right now. The truth is you may never feel ready to join the journey. Even while on the journey, the hardest step is always the next one. John Piper, who is admired by so many in this generation for his boldness and passion, says, as to his life's prayer, *"Lord, let me make a difference for you that is utterly disproportionate to who I am."* He still doesn't feel ready, and the inside secret is—no one does. We must answer the calling of our time. There is no time to hesitate, or we will find ourselves frozen with the others who are without a God–given vision for their life. The greatest danger is not that you will mess it up or fail, but that you will do nothing. The bystander apathy of the church has crippled the work of the Great Commission far too long. It is today that a generation must volunteer their lives to God's global purpose no matter what the cost. God has a purpose for your life. You were set apart from the beginning, so that your life would write the crucial last pages of the story of all God is doing. Now that you have seen the North Star and the compass of God's heart, hear the Word of the Lord for you.

"Remember the former things long past, for I am God, and there is no one like Me, declaring the end from the beginning ... saying, 'My purpose will be established, and I will accomplish all My good pleasure'; calling ... the man of My purpose from a far country. I will bring it to pass. I have planned it, surely I will do it" (Isaiah 46:9–11).

The gospel has come to you to connect your life with a story and a purpose bigger than yourself. Now the gospel is on its way through you to the ends of the earth. You were created for this one journey. Take your next step.

---

1. Erwin McManus, *Seizing Your Divine Moment*, Thomas Nelson Publishers, 2002, p42.
2. Navigator, vol. 2, #8, April, 1999.

livelifeonpurpose

God's Purpose.   Your Life.   One Journey.

Ordering Information:
1–877–421–READ (7323)
www.winepresssbooks.com
Also available at: www.amazon.com

For bulk orders send an email to:
livelifeonpurpose@thetravelingteam.org
Or Call: 1.888.467.8866

Scheduling / Speaking
Contact Information for Claude Hickman
The Traveling Team
PO Box 567
Conway, AR 72033
1.888.467.8866
claude@thertravelingteam.org

Websites to help you continue living purposefully:
www.thetravelingteam.org
www.thebodybuilders.net
www.stumo.org
www.perspectives.org
www.rightnow.org